"This book asks why so ma
outdated, counterproducti·

Today's world is chan
businesses must do likewise if they are to succeed ...
economy.

The cost of this book may be the best investment you make
this year."

Jeremy Dale, VP, Marketing, Motorola

"Too many companies are stuck in the Stone Age. And too
many leaders aren't willing to speak that simple truth. Thank
heaven, then, for Sally Bibb. Her book is a badly needed call to
make our organizations more effective by making them more
humane."

Daniel H. Pink, author of A WHOLE NEW MIND
and FREE AGENT NATION

"The persistence of the myth of organizations as solid,
structured edifices with a man at the top in control, holding
things together with rules and procedures, has always
fascinated me.

If the myth was ever true those days are long gone, and in
this book Sally Bibb gets into the guts of why it is such
nonsense and how we can set about revealing the true nature
of organizations as groups of willing individuals held together
by a common purpose and trust in each other."

Euan Semple, Director, KM Solutions, BBC

"So many businesses go to the wall because they refuse to
change their belief in archaic ways of managing. Sally plots a
new course for decent modern enterprise. She challenges the
basis of what many obese and aging companies stand for, in a

clear and refreshing manner. Nice to hear some plain talk in a business book for once."

Dan Germain, Creative Director, Innocent Drinks

"Reading this book makes me glad to work for a progressive company like Dyson."

Martin McCourt, CEO, Dyson Ltd

"In future, sustainable performance and growth will depend on people changing the paradigms with which they work. Sally Bibb's analysis gives us all a challenge on how to effect personal change which will support this initiative. I believe a focus on values and greater emotional courage can make a difference. Education and business should consider how to accept and implement this challenge."

Bill Colquhoun, formerly Vice President,
Shell Chemicals Ltd

"Some people think businesses are impersonal efficiency machines. They need to be efficient but the only way to succeed is to make the world of work a place for real humans. As Sally points out, good people who are trusted in a values driven environment are the recipe for business success!"

Richard Davies, Human Resources Director, SABMiller Europe

"Sally has cut to the core of the constant migration of people from one company to another and one business to another searching for an environment in which they may flourish. If companies really believe they are investors in people then this book is well worth a read by every manager at every level."

Jonathan Fontaine, Area Manager, Lloyds TSB Group

THE STONE AGE COMPANY

The Stone Age Company

Why the companies we work for are dying and how they can be saved

Sally Bibb

CYAN

Marshall Cavendish
Business

Copyright © 2005 Sally Bibb

First published in 2005 by:

Marshall Cavendish Business
An imprint of Marshall Cavendish International (Asia) Private Limited
A member of Times Publishing Limited
Times Centre, 1 New Industrial Road
Singapore 536196
T: +65 6213 9300
F: +65 6285 4871
E: te@sg.marshallcavendish.com
Online bookstore: www.marshallcavendish.com/genref

and

Cyan Communications Limited
119 Wardour Street
London W1F 0UW
United Kingdom
T: +44 (0)20 7565 6120
E: sales@cyanbooks.com
www.cyanbooks.com

A CIP record for this book is available from the British Library

ISBN 981 261 823 6 (Asia & ANZ)
ISBN 1-904879-43-8 (Rest of world)

Designed and typeset by Curran Publishing Services, Norwich, UK
Printed and bound in Singapore

I dedicate this book to Keaton and Cerys.

I hope that when they are old enough to work
they find themselves amongst enlightened
people in enlightened organizations.

Contents

Tables

Acknowledgments

Writing this book has been fun. Working with Martin Liu of Cyan Books has made it more so. He's a real pro and it is a great education working with him. Also huge thanks to Pom who is not only brilliant at what she does but is also a real joy to work with.

For helping me to get on the road to writing and introducing me to Martin I thank Jeremy Kourdi.

To the other authors in the series, Susan and Adrian, thanks for joining me in this pursuit. It's always fun and the wine is always good!

Thank you to Andy Maslen whose love of writing is contagious. He has coached me and helped me to understand and appreciate the craft.

For introducing me to new worlds and ideas I thank Gerard Fairtlough, Karen Otazo, Julia Rowntree, and Barbara Heinzen.

My family and friends, as usual, have been amazing. In their own special ways they give my life and work so much meaning. For your encouragement and interest in my writing thank you mum, Jamie, Auntie Jean, Auntie Sylvia, Andy, Anna, Ali, Ceris, Elaine, Geoff, Grania, Jonathan, Kate, Margot, Mark, Marie, Mary, Ron, Shaun, Stephen, Sue, Susan, Vicky, and all my other friends who have been there for me to talk, eat, drink, and dance with in the midst of all the work.

For your generosity, time, honesty, and excellent editing, thank you, Ali.

For being such an inspiration, a wise teacher, and for being a leader that I want to follow I thank David Laird.

Last but not least, for always believing in me, nurturing my interest in the world, and for knowing that I could be whatever I wanted to be, I thank my dad.

Sally Bibb

Introduction

The truth is ... that businesses are totally outdated in the way they are run. Hierarchy and controlling ways of managing are based on the old-fashioned view that people have to be kept under careful watch and tight control at work. What nonsense! Yet businesses rarely question this way of working. Why? Because it is beneficial to those highest up in the hierarchy who are earning the most money and getting the most privileges. Why would they want to change things?

I have been writing this book in my head for several years. Mostly my views, observations, and ideas have come about as a result of frustration about what I have experienced myself or heard about from friends and colleagues. I have witnessed some astonishingly awful behavior from managers—people who are supposed to be the leaders and role models in organizations. I have also been amazed at how irrational decisions and ways of working are dressed up and justified as the sensible way forward. This is real Emperor's new clothes stuff.

More recently though I have encountered organizations that are reinventing the way businesses are run. I have met leaders who are inspiring. They have a vision and are clear what they are about, what they believe in, and what they want to achieve. Admittedly I haven't met many of them. Maybe that is all the more reason that they stand out and why they have impressed me. They strike me as being "whole" in a way that many leaders I have met are not. Most of us have known the uninspiring types of leader. They can be uninspiring for many reasons. Some seem colorless, lacking passion, conviction, and imagination. Some are wimpy and weak.

Others are driven by insecurity; they spend their time sucking up to the people above them. Maybe they are terribly ambitious and hungry for their own scraps of power. Or maybe they are just ingratiating and get a feeling of worth by being associated with those more powerful.

We have probably all known our fair share of managers like these in our time. They appear to be wearing a mask, playing a role. Psychologists would say that at an unconscious level they are desperately trying to prove to themselves (usually because they had to prove themselves to their parents) that they are worthy and successful. It's obvious who they are. Sometimes it's the ones who appear to be the most confident. Underneath they are making a desperate quest to prove themselves over and over again. They operate out of ambition and ego.

These are the people who certainly don't inspire me and I would never want to follow them.

These types of people, working in the kind of companies that need, promote, and rely on them and their dysfunctional behavior, are a dying breed. They have to be. Why? Because the world is changing. People are becoming more savvy. All matters psychological, once the preserve of the few and definitely not something that organizations particularly considered, are more mainstream and known about. Personal development courses, counseling, and psychotherapy—all have shed the stigma, even become fashionable activities for some. There are many, many companies that employ (and listen to) psychologists, use psychometric tests as a way of assessing people for jobs, and try to make the organization a better place to work. It is increasingly common for companies to talk about values. For most it's lip service but it is significant that they are realizing that values are important to their customers and the people who work for them.

The point is, that at some level the people who run companies today are realizing that things need to change. (Fewer of course are realizing that they themselves need to change.) In most cases they are making half-hearted, ham-fisted attempts to change their companies. Usually there is a lack of genuine desire, let alone wherewithal to do it. So what the workers see are lots of initiatives, good words, and spin. They don't see much honesty and genuine effort.

However, I am an optimistic person and I think I have seen enough evidence to suggest that the next generation will have a very different experience of organizations than the one that most people who are reading this book will have had.

I hope that this age, in the early part of the noughties, will in the not too distant future be known as the time when a step-change occurred in evolution in the world of organizations. There will be name for the change as there has been for other major times of change such as the Industrial Revolution. Perhaps it will be called something like "the post-rational era," or "the humanizing of work and business," because that is exactly what it is. The less enlightened leaders see the world of business as either/or; either you can be nice to your staff or you can make money for your shareholders.

I will never forget a conversation I had recently with a leader of a large business. We were talking about the appalling behavior of one of his senior managers. He said "Well, we can be nice to people or we can make money," as if they were diametrically opposed. The worst thing was that even when I challenged his statement he couldn't see the flaw. His belief system, like that of many leaders, is that you have to be mean and hard to do good business; anything else is soft. HR might insist you do it, but you can make more money by being tough and having a tight control on everything, including the people.

I will show in this book why leaders have to think differently, and why in fact developing shareholder value is too narrow a concept.

My reason for writing this book is that I want to encourage those who are pioneering change. I want to contribute to changing our experience of organizations, both as customers and employees. Of course the pioneers probably don't need much encouragement. They have a belief and a cause that keeps them going. These are people like the guys who set up the Innocent drink company in the United Kingdom. A tiny company who have a fairly unremarkable product line—juices and smoothies; strong values, and an unconventional way of running their business. They have had so much publicity, been written up in numerous management magazines and books, and were even invited to meet Tony Blair to share the secrets of their success. It's fantastic that they have had that kind of exposure and recognition, but I hope that in the next five to ten years stories like theirs will become so common that they are no longer newsworthy in the same way. Their way of running business will be the norm. It will be the corporations with archaic, unfriendly ways that will be the odd ones out.

1

Clutching at straws: A picture of the Stone Age company

Most of us work in organizations of some form or another. We spend an increasing amount of our lives in them. What sort of places are they? Are they places within which we really thrive? Some are. Far, far more are not.

It is time to take a look at these organizations. We need to question the unquestioned and to challenge our deeply held assumptions about how they should be run.

Having worked in organizations for years I have seen what great places they can be, and I have also seen how stifling and unpleasant they can be at times. I have been amazed by the success that results when people trust one another and collaborate. However, I have also observed much that doesn't work within companies. I have witnessed the frustration and anger that arise in companies that have outdated practices, are slow to change, and view people as production units, not as human beings. My term for these types of companies is "Stone Age."

I felt compelled to write this book because there is so much that isn't working and so much that needs to change. The views I express in this book are borne of my own observations, experience, reading and many conversations, over years, with people who are dissatisfied with the environment within which they work. Most people I know and talk to who work in organizations are critical of them. Far fewer are happy, inspired, optimistic, and positive about the companies they work for. But there are companies out there that are great places to work and to do business with. There may be fewer of them but they are increasing in number. And they are successful. So what makes the difference? That is what I am going to examine in this book.

I am not naturally cynical; I usually see the upside of most situations. In recent years, though, I have found myself increasingly questioning what goes on in companies. The impetus for writing this book has come from a belief that the Stone Age company's time has come and gone. I believe that we now need to look clearly and objectively at companies, at what's working, what's not working, and what the alternative is.

I am optimistic about the future. I believe that companies will, over time, become better places. The impetus for this is that an increasing number of people are being instinctively drawn towards what I call "enlightened" companies.

This book is an attempt to provide a different framework to think about organizations. In the course of writing it I have talked to many people at different levels in companies. Some have been shocked at my views, others have been angry about some of the things I have said. These have usually been senior people. Others have been pleased and relieved that I am shaking the tree. No one has been indifferent. All of them have wanted to engage in the debate. I hope that you, reader, will be stimulated into either agreeing or disagreeing with what I say. I hope that it will provoke questions and debate. But most of all I hope that you will be inspired by stories of the positive and the possibilities for a different type of company: a company that thrills its customers, that is innovative and efficient, and that is fun and energizing to work for.

THE EMPEROR'S NEW CLOTHES

I was recently wandering around a business in London. The outside of the building was an impressive monolith of marble and glass. Judging by outside appearances, it was a business of the modern age. Inside, however, was a different matter. First came the layout. The senior people had offices of varying sizes depending, I assume, on their position in the hierarchy. The rest were seated in a variety of stalls with screens between them. I had to smile and remember a time almost 20 years ago when I first started working. It was exactly the same—well, not exactly. There was less gleaming chrome and glass, and the wood was darker. The square footage of floor space you got was directly related to your seniority. Really! It was bizarre. But it was the way things were done then and no one questioned it. The really scary thing is that it is still the way things are done in many businesses. In a way it is worse than it was, because the conversation about size of office and square footage doesn't happen nowadays, but the allocation of privilege based on position still does. It's just that we don't admit that that's what it is about. Power and privilege are still the determinants of who gets what. It is still one of those facts of business life that few people ever openly question. Like the fact that women were once not able to vote; for a long time no one challenged it but now we can't believe that it took so long for the obvious anachronism to change.

So why aren't things like these questioned? Well, let's face it. Who is going to question them? It's highly unlikely to be the managers themselves who are enjoying the privileges. Why would they? And the ones who don't are less powerful, so they probably wouldn't dare, even if it occurred to them. And even if they did, who would listen to them?

Why am I talking about size of offices? Is it really that important? Does it matter? It matters because it is a symptom. It is a sign of the fact that nothing much has changed, and businesses and the people in them are still preoccupied with issues of status and power instead of getting on with what they are there for.

Office space isn't the only symptom of a Stone Age organization. Have a look at the list below. It is full of things that we accept and we don't question. Maybe you recognize some from companies you have worked in. These are the kind of characteristics we find in the Stone Age company.

- The decision makers are at the top of the hierarchy— usually farthest away from all the information and insight that will help them to make a decision.
- People are paid more according to how high they are in the hierarchy (irrespective of what they contribute).
- People must have managers irrespective of how competent, experienced, and confident they are.
- The best specialists or technicians are promoted into management positions that they may have neither the will nor ability to do well.
- Difficult, badly behaved people get to keep their jobs when good people lose theirs.
- CEOs rarely give a straight answer.
- At meetings people don't usually say what they want

to say even though often everyone knows what needs to be said.

- At meetings if everyone agrees it is usually because at least one person is not saying what he really thinks.
- Bosses think they know everything—otherwise why do they never admit they made a mistake?
- Companies spend a lot of time and money getting managers to do appraisals that make absolutely no difference to performance and very often result in the person concerned feeling demotivated.
- It is assumed that managers know more than the staff themselves do about how good they are, as it's the managers who do the appraisals.
- We work with someone as a colleague and when she gets promoted into a senior position we start to treat her differently: not being so open with the person, not saying what we really think, feeling nervous about what she thinks of us.
- We sometimes even assume that people higher up in the hierarchy are somehow better than us!
- Companies spend a lot of time and money designing incentive schemes that don't act as an incentive at all.
- Annual objectives are set, but they become obsolete within weeks and are rarely revisited until appraisal time.
- Frequently promotion is based upon current performance, not upon the ability to carry out a more senior role.
- Corporate social responsibility is usually just a PR exercise, and often cynically exploited as a type of brand marketing.

- People aren't interested in changing things. They are scared of challenging the corporate wisdom. They want to pretend that the Emperor *does* have new clothes, because the alternative is just too risky. They compromise their integrity every day.
- People tell their partners more about what is wrong with their company than they tell their boss or colleagues.
- People are more preoccupied with themselves than with their customers.

PROGRESS? WHAT PROGRESS?

Despite the wisdom of many management writers and consultants, the list above is depressingly the state of many businesses today. This way of running companies emerged in the post-Industrial Revolution period when the majority of industry was based on manufacturing. People worked on production lines. There were lots of men and women doing menial tasks. Each of their tasks was part of a bigger process to produce something. These were the days of time and motion study when, in the work context, a human being was treated as a machine. The job of time and motion people was to analyze exactly what, how, and how long an individual took to do something. The analysis was used to figure out ways of making individuals more efficient by changing the way they did part or all of the task, shaving off time, changing their position on the production line, and so on.

Of course, the flaw in this whole way of thinking was that human beings are not machines. They are unpredictable. The behavior and motivation of people are dependent on many and varied factors that just can't be predicted and controlled. The irony is that the early ways of thinking about controlling and managing people have stuck, and they are still at the base of much of our management practice today. True, it has become a little more sophisticated and taken account of the "intelligent worker," but the core belief that people can't be trusted and need to be monitored and controlled is still very much alive and thriving. It is still behind all sorts of management and HR practices. Take job evaluation schemes. Most of them do take account of the fact that people need to have judgment in their jobs, and few jobs today can be prescribed exactly. However, one only has to examine the reasons that job evaluation is done in the first place to realize that it is still rooted in outdated beliefs about the nature of work and the worker in the modern world.

THE ASSUMPTION THAT PEOPLE CAN'T BE TRUSTED

That, I am afraid to say, is the premise behind much management practice. So much time is spent preparing job descriptions that detail exactly what has to be done, how it has to be done, what decisions people can and can't make, who they are accountable to, and who is accountable to them. Irrespective of people's backgrounds, experience, and skills, no matter how much they are paid, they must have a job description. Typically the job description is put away and not looked at again until the job holder leaves and someone else is hired to do exactly the same job. In reality people make their jobs what they want them to be. They do as much as possible of the things they enjoy and as little as possible of the things they don't. They find ways of papering over areas of the job that they are not very good at. Maybe they get someone else to do certain bits for them in a barter arrangement. All sorts of "renegotiation" and blurring of the boundaries take place. Are managers stupid not to realize that they are wasting their time producing job descriptions, or are they simply in denial? The truth is that they don't really think about it.

THINKING—A DANGEROUS AND RARE PASTIME

You would be forgiven for thinking that managers don't use their brains very much. If they really sat down and thought about why they spend so much time on things like putting together job descriptions they would surely realize the banality of it. If you can, think of your own job description. You probably can't. You do the job you do in the way that helps you to feel as motivated and competent as possible. Or, look at it this way: Would it make any difference to your performance if you didn't have a job description? I doubt it.

What's the big deal with job descriptions, and why am I spending so much time talking about them? The big deal is that they are a symptom of the fact that people that run companies do unnecessary things to make them feel as if they are in control.

THE ILLUSION OF BEING IN CONTROL

Have you ever done one of those psychometric tests that tells you what sort of a person you are at work, and goes into things like what motivates you? They are so common nowadays. In fact firms of psychologists have built a massive and lucrative industry out of them. Between them, they have norm groups and psychological profiles of thousands of managers all over the world. The fact that managers have a psychological need for power and control is a well-known, well-documented fact. It is accepted as good that they are driven that way. Otherwise they might not be strong leaders. Right?

Wrong. The fact that so many heads of companies and senior managers are driven by power and control explains why companies today, unless they change radically, are going to die. The psychological profile of those who are running these companies means that they are genetically predisposed not to evolve. And we know from nature what happens when organisms are incapable of evolving.

EVOLVE OR DIE

So where is the impetus for change coming from? If business leaders don't change themselves, they won't be able to change their companies. In the Stone Age company change doesn't come from the leaders. To be different is to stand out and, to go back to the analogy with nature; anyone who is different is either forced into line or forced out. There is an unspoken, often unconscious, code at play in these powerhouses at the top of organizations. I used to think that people at that level of companies must be more talented, more clever, and in some indefinable way better than the rest of us mortals. Now I know that is not true. What they often are is more adept at sounding confident, more driven by power, more ambitious, and better at hiding their insecurities than the rest of us. And because others collude with them, they manage to stay in senior positions and get promoted too, because they understand power and they are usually very good at sucking up to the boss in whatever way their particular boss likes to be sucked up to.

More than once I have been in meetings with very senior people and their bosses, and been amazed and disgusted at the blatant sycophancy. When I first witnessed this, I wondered why the boss didn't realize, and somehow signal that she was not impressed by this behavior. After a while it dawned on me that the boss probably did realize, and enjoyed the fact that she was having this effect on these people. It is all just a game to make bosses feel good, and therefore protect or promote themselves or their position. When I witness scenes like this I don't know whether to feel sorry for these people or angry with them. They have sold themselves out and, as far as I am concerned, have compromised their integrity for scraps of power. How enlightened and clever is that? And these are the people who are running our corporations today.

DENIAL—THE BIG MANAGEMENT DISEASE

So why do senior managers persist in doing things that sustain Stone Age companies? The answer may lie in the fact that they are in denial. Denial is a useful protective mechanism. Some might say it is understandable that they close their eyes to what is really going on because what's the alternative? The alternative is often facing up to difficult truths. And those speaking the truth run the risk of being marginalized in some way. Just in case it's crossing your mind that I am exaggerating or dramatizing, think about it. If I put forward this point of view to the people concerned they would deny it vehemently. Groups of people have very powerful ways of maintaining the status quo and sticking to the rules of the game. You see it in any kind of organization, whether it is a prison, a family, or a boardroom. Human beings are hard-wired to do what it takes to survive and fit into their "tribe," even if that tribe has no loyalty for them whatsoever. The rules of the game are intricate and complex, and woe betide those who flout them.

We see this behavior in all sorts of situations. There was a famous experiment done by psychologists. They took a group of student volunteers and randomly split them into two groups. One group was told they had to pretend they were prisoners, and the other group that they were prison officers. Even though they knew that they were part of an experiment, they started to assume the roles. The psychologists had to stop the experiment because the prison officers started abusing the prisoners. Some prisoners started to behave nastily to other prisoners and started acting in a subservient way towards the prison officers. When questioned after the experiment, the majority of the prison "officers" said that they didn't want to behave in that way, but they felt pressurized to do so by the group.

You see the same thing in a much milder form in all sorts of situations, such as juries or groups of women at a toddlers' group. People don't want to stand out, get it wrong, and be picked on by others. They go along with those more powerful, and contribute to the status quo. The consequences of this can be horrific, the most disgusting example of course being the holocaust. Of course not all German officers and soldiers were evil people, but they did go into denial in a big way, and colluded with an appalling set of rules and norms. If they hadn't, Hitler would never have managed to do what he did.

Of course, consequences are nowhere near as severe when we are talking about companies, but plenty of injustices have been done because people have not spoken up for fear of repercussions and the reaction of the boss or their peer group.

This is insidious behavior that has caused the downfall of people from their jobs and careers, and has of course also caused the spectacular downfall of companies. And all because people who could speak up didn't have the guts or the integrity to do so.

ALL YOU NEED TO LEARN ABOUT MANAGEMENT YOU LEARNT IN THE SCHOOLYARD

Relatively few people evolve very much emotionally and psychologically during their lifetime. What they learn to do is to play the game and employ social and political skills to survive in the adult world. Actually, though, most individuals are not that different as adults from how they were as children. They carry around the same emotional hurts and insecurities, they are still trying to gain approval and recognition. When we were children it was our parents or the people who brought us up to whom we tried to prove ourselves. Even when we get to be responsible and successful adults, that unconscious drive is still very strong. It is not something most people are aware of. It is just part of their psychological make-up. I would say that the majority of people do not ask themselves why they are as they are. However, thankfully, there is a growing understanding and recognition of the part that psychology plays in the making or breaking of relationships and businesses. Several contemporary CEOs have acknowledged openly what they are made of and why they are as they are.

Larry Ellison, the founder and CEO of Oracle, knows that his drive and determination comes from a drive to prove himself because his father told him "You will never amount to anything." It is particularly commonplace in boys to try all their lives to prove themselves to their fathers. It continues even after their father has died, so strong is the drive and so ingrained is it in the person's psyche. It can be a positive force and it can be a destructive force. Look at George W. Bush. It is said that he is trying to prove himself and live up to the deep-seated effects of being brought up by a dominant mother and a father compared with whom he has a lot to live up to.

Understanding this really does shed light on what happens in the executive suite. Every time I witness executives at work, interacting with each other, throwing their weight around, and trying to prove themselves to their bosses, I see the little child in each of them doing that when they were young. It doesn't take too much imagination to do this.

A couple of years ago I organized a day for children who were doing work experience. They ranged between 8 and 11 years old. I had them do all sorts of management training exercises. These were exercises that were designed to help them to see what role they naturally played in teams, what they were particularly good at, and how they got on with others. It was fascinating to watch. There was the bossy, dominant one who never listened to others, the conciliator who tried to resolve conflict that arose in the group, the shy one who didn't assert himself much at all even though he clearly had something to offer. They were all there, all the types that you see in any kind of organization every day. I reckoned that if I could have turned the clock forward 30 years I would have recognized each one of them. The things that drove them to behave in the ways they did were firmly established already at that young age, and for most people that would be how they would run their lives for the rest of their lives, whether or not this kind of behavior would make them happy, help them to build effective relationships, or help them to get what they wanted from their lives or not. This is hard-wiring.

There are no prizes for guessing which types would have ended up in the executive suite. Of course it would have been the arrogant, dominant, egotistical ones. These are the types that still dominate the boardroom. There are exceptions, of course, and there are companies that are run by the modest, thoughtful types who are highly skilled in developing relationships and who are not driven to prove themselves. They are still relatively rare, but they are becoming more common. I take a look at some of them later on in this book.

THE CONSEQUENCES OF OVERGROWN SCHOOLKIDS RUNNING COMPANIES

Have you ever noticed what happens when school children fall out with each other? They don't have the skills to resolve conflict. Their options are limited to joining another gang, changing their "best friends," or fighting to "win" the argument and forcing the other kid to either fight or to retreat. What happens as kids get older and start working in companies? They still resort to name-calling, trying to eject someone from their gang, and changing allegiances. The "grown-up" way of doing all this is called "politics." Usually there are no teachers to spot what is going on and stop it. There are only older kids who have more power and probably enjoy watching the younger ones fight it out.

It is fascinating to watch executives through this lens. I remember a meeting where a particularly arrogant executive who had been given a lot of power was publicly asked to do something by his boss. He refused. He sat there with his arms folded. A hush descended on the room. The boss capitulated and gave a reason why indeed it was not a good idea for him to do the thing that he had just been asked to do. If you put the same situation into the classroom you would see the arrogant, rebellious little boy defiantly disobeying the teacher. This particular teacher is nervous of the boy. In fact, most of the teachers are. So he would get away with it, and over time get more and more sense of his own power, and become more and more arrogant until someone "bigger" than him knocked him down a peg or two. Certainly this is unsophisticated, dysfunctional, immature behavior. My experience is that the higher you go up a company's hierarchy, the more you see this kind of behavior. I no longer think that those who run companies are somehow superior to the rest of us. They are just particularly driven by power, and good at appearing confident and bluffing.

SMART PEOPLE ARE OVERRATED

According to psychologists, the best predictor of success for executives is intelligence. Even after Daniel Goleman (*Emotional Intelligence*, 1999, Bloomsbury) educated us about the importance of emotional intelligence, we still think of intelligence as "brainpower." Emotional intelligence is still not widely viewed as a strength or asset. Even though occupational psychologists measure it and talk about it, and it is a concept that is understood, it is still not seen as essential. It is rarely even seen as an asset.

Companies make the mistake of attributing so-called intelligent people with lots of other positive qualities. They assume they will be the best at the job. However, having intelligence doesn't mean that people use it well. If they did, people with MBAs would always be the best business leaders. But of course they are not. They have just accumulated lots of knowledge and management know-how. It does not teach them how to be better leaders. In fact it can often appear that the more intelligent they are, the less they seem to be able to relate to and motivate people. Of course there are people who are very bright and emotionally sophisticated, and capable too. Somehow or other, not many of them find their way to very senior positions in companies.

I was recently talking to an unusually wise HR manager about how most companies handle redundancies. We agreed that more often than not they focus on the process, not on the people. He said something that I wish more HR people realized. He said that when you make people redundant, the thing that they remember is how you made them feel. Even the most rational and hard-nosed person is susceptible to feelings under such circumstances. Until they get a taste of their own medicine, of course, most managers don't care about feelings.

I remember one manager who had made lots of people redundant in his career. He always did it in a businesslike and professional way, and he always made the right kind of supportive comments. However, what was startlingly obvious was that he had no empathy at all for these people. Making them redundant was just one of the more unpleasant tasks that he had to perform in his career. He was a positive man, someone who always saw opportunities to learn, no matter how tough the route to learning. One of the ways that he coped with having to make and carry out these tough decisions was to tell himself that it made him a better manager. (To him that equaled more marketable!) I should emphasize that he wasn't an unpleasant person. On the contrary, he was affable, pleasant to work with, thoughtful, and concerned about treating people in the right way. However, two things got in his way. One was his inability to genuinely empathize with these people. The other was his own anxiety when he was dealing with people in such tough situations. So he was never totally "with them" during the conversation, because he was wrapped up in his own nervousness about how they would react, could he handle their reaction, would they hate him, and so on. Much of this was unconscious, of course, but it got in the way.

People do pick up if you are genuinely listening to them or not, or if your intention is to get it over with as quickly as possible because it's an uncomfortable situation to be in. Really great leaders feel those kind of feelings too, but the difference is that they are aware of them and can manage them. This level of self-awareness is rare.

The manager I referred to suddenly got a big dose of self-awareness and a sudden empathy implant when he himself was made redundant. His emotional reaction (anger followed by a huge feeling of loss) was so acute that he could barely communicate with anyone for several weeks. Suddenly he *understood*. Afterwards he told me that he had understood before, but only theoretically. Now he understood because he had had the experience. He said it was very humbling and "one of the most important growth experiences" he had had as a leader.

THE LIMITATIONS OF LOGIC

There are some jobs where pure intelligence is really important, of course: strategists' and analysts' jobs, for instance. The trouble is that what happens is that these people are often given leadership responsibilities too. So they need to be able to apply their cleverness to those challenges. You may assume that that would work. The funny thing is that clever people often apply only logic to organizational problems, and think that is all they need to do. Emotional intelligence and an understanding of people are obviously crucial as well.

I have seen it time and time again in situations that call for excellent leadership skills, such as when organizations are being restructured and people are being made redundant. What happens is that management work out what they want to do, and these days they might sit down with the HR person and work out how to communicate the changes. The first problem is that they are almost always averse to telling it as it is. Messages about organizational changes are rarely without corporate-speak, spin, and euphemism. I have participated in many meetings to discuss communications. The most hilarious part is often the part where someone suggests doing an FAQ (frequently asked questions). Managers who don't really care at all what people are going to think and feel can't be bothered to put the effort into thinking about what people might ask or want to know. To do that would mean that they would have to try to put themselves into those people's shoes for a while, and think about life from their point of view. Most have absolutely no interest in doing that, even if they are capable of doing it. When badgered into it by the HR person, they leave the really tricky questions out, and fudge the answers to the difficult questions. FAQs rarely tell you anything that helps to promote understanding of the situation at hand.

Really arrogant, power-hungry managers don't even consider explaining their rationale for the changes. The ones who do, or are persuaded by HR that it is a good idea, think that explaining their rationale in the barest of terms is all they need to do to get people to buy into the changes. The emotionally incompetent manager who has no under-standing of human beings or how to manage change thinks that to explain the rationale is enough to gain acceptance. Despite all the theory and case studies about how to manage change effectively, organizations almost always do it badly. Why? In a nutshell, it's because the leaders don't care about doing it well, and HR people don't care either. They don't know how to manage change, nor do they have the clout to influence how it is done. It is truly astonishing how terrible some companies are at this. Table 1.1 shows the effective versus the ineffective ways to manage change. The effective way is as simple as the ineffective way but rarely chosen as an option.

TABLE 1.1 MANAGING CHANGE:
THE GOOD, THE BAD/THE UGLY

The good	The bad/ugly
■ Tell people what's going on	■ Only tell people what they have to
■ Are open and honest	■ Are secretive
■ Treat employees like adults	■ Treat them like children
■ Communicate clearly	■ Spin the story
■ Involve people/ ask their opinion	■ Make decisions based on top people's limited knowledge
■ Explain their thinking and rationale	■ Just tell them the bare facts
■ Welcome questions and challenges	■ Dictate how it is going to be
■ Admit when something isn't working and change it	■ Never admit they are wrong

It's amazing that so many intelligent leaders manage change badly. It is hard to see why when you examine the logic behind the "bad" approach and the likely consequences. The logic, such as it is, is that people will do as they are told and they don't need to be involved. The intention is not to manage the change well and get maximum support from employees; it is to do it quickly. It is enough for most managers just to get it done and to be able to tell their boss that it's done, irrespective of how it is done or the effects on employees and customers. Most managers simply don't care about the "how." All they care about is that anything that is valued by their boss and can be seen by their boss is done well. The truth is that what bosses value is results. They don't care about how they are achieved, only that they are.

Take the case of the autocratic sales manager who threatens her senior staff that if they don't bring in the numbers this month they will have to start looking for another job. They in turn pass that threat on to their staff. The staff don't know what else to do to bring in the numbers, so they start to call customers and say something like this: "We're desperate to make our targets this month. You haven't got another £4,000 in your budget that you could spend with us, have you?" What sort of impression does this give to customers? The manager either didn't think about that, or doesn't care. All the manager cares about is making her targets so that she can look good. In this particular case it is ego gone mad.

As long as things look OK on the surface, then that is fine. It is astonishing to me that even though there is a high risk that the company's reputation could be seriously damaged by this kind of behavior if it got out and/or someone sued, it is still tolerated. This really begins to look like a serious lack of integrity. These bosses have survived and thrived for so long without being challenged that they have become unassailable. It is a very dangerous state of affairs. So much for corporate governance. Integrity, transparency, and ethics in business affect the efficiency and success of companies, but unethical behavior persists in many companies.

Senior managers who lead with integrity, who do what is right and don't succumb to their own egos, are the exception. They stand out because they are still such an unusual breed. In my almost 20 years of working I have met less than a dozen people like this, and only worked with two of them. You could think of that as either depressing or hopeful. I think of it as hopeful because there is such a major crisis of trust in business and politics today, people are starting to value leaders like this. They are going to become a premium product.

Let me tell you the story of one of the two. I worked with him a long time ago, long before I started to understand organizations and how they work. However, I did realize that he stood out as being very different from his peers. There were many, many examples of that. Here is one of them.

I shall call him Steve for the purposes of this story. One night I went into his office. I had made a big mistake that was going to cost the company £20,000 a day until it was fixed. This was my first encounter with Steve. He was the only senior manager left in the building that evening, so I had no choice but to go to him. Together we fixed the problem, and all was well by the next morning. That was not the point. The thing I will always remember about that incident was how he handled it.

He was on the phone to his wife when I first walked into his office, telling her he would be home for supper soon. He signaled to me that it was no problem for me to wait. I told him about my mistake. He listened, and asked me lots of questions in an inquiring way, not in an accusatory way. It was this that made me realize he was genuinely trying to understand, and that he would work with me, not blame me. Indeed he did work with me. He was a top manager and I was very junior. We worked late and solved the problem between us. But what he taught me that night was a huge lesson that has lasted and stood me in good stead in my career ever since. He taught me about integrity, about doing the right thing, and about how to get the best out of people and create trust.

As I got to know him better I realized that he was the only senior manager in that company who really knew what was going on, because staff and customers talked honestly to him. The industry was one where things went wrong often. That was just its nature. He probably saved the company millions (not to mention many customer relationships) because people were honest with him, and staff and customers wanted to help him. It was also a heavily unionized environment. He had no problems. Some of his colleagues were always at war with the unions.

When I was an HR manager I had countless conversations with bosses who believed you have to be tough and mean to be able to manage well. To them it was black and white. Either you were tough and mean or you were soft and a pushover. Steve was no pushover but he was fair. You don't have to be mean to be a strong and effective leader. There was no one else in that company with his leadership ability, and as I said earlier, I have only worked with one other since.

How many leaders like Steve do you know? He did what he instinctively knew was right. The last thing on his mind was how he would look or his own ambition. I always admired him greatly because he spoke up. Years after the incident I mentioned above I told him what it had meant to me and what an impact it had had on the way I view management. He told me that it had not been easy at times to be like he was. It almost cost him his career on a number of occasions, but he is the sort of person who couldn't not do the right thing.

Some of his colleagues along the way distanced themselves from him and betrayed him. There were a few who deliberately did things to try to bring about his downfall, but in the end, when the company was in a very difficult position he was the one who stuck his neck out and sorted out problems that no one else could. Those who had been his enemies were thankful. All of them changed their attitude completely, and now they respect and admire him, albeit some of them do so grudgingly. Steve had so strong a sense of what was right and just. He has been hugely successful because not only is he very competent but, more than that, people trust him. He has integrity and he also will admit when he is wrong. That can be risky for senior people. I asked him about this and why he chose to do it. He told me that he never thought about it being a choice. It is just the way he is. He is very sure about his values and what is important to him. He is a legend in his field among colleagues and customers alike. When his name is mentioned, people always come up with many stories about what a great guy he is, and what he achieved. The stories are never told without the person talking about what they admire about him. How many senior leaders evoke that response?

WHEN THEY WANT TO FOLLOW

Steve was a boss who people wanted to follow. They didn't always like what he did or the decisions he made, but they trusted him. They knew that his intentions were always good. He listened to them and he respected their views. Many years have passed since I worked with him. The details of what we worked on and the daily life of that company are now extremely hazy in my memory. However, the impact of working with him has stuck, and has influenced who I am as a leader. I learnt so much from him. I learnt things that you can never learn in business school. What is more, there are not too many people out there who are able to teach those things. This is a huge gap in the capability of companies today. They have few role-model leaders who can pass their wisdom down. When it happens it is very powerful.

I know of a man in business now who is a bit like Steve. He has a very clear vision that he communicates well. Bad leaders often do so too. The difference with this guy is that he leads people by listening, giving them direction and support when they need it, helping them, and mentoring them. Even though he has now left the business, they still call him to talk through problems. He is always having real, two-way conversations that keep people involved. The funny thing is when I talked to him about this, he was very modest. He didn't understand how good he was. It reminded me of the research that Jim Collins did and published in his 2001 book *Good to Great* (HarperCollins). He talks about leadership and the best leaders being the modest unassuming types not the charismatic, minor celebrity types. He said that one of the things that really great leaders do when things go right is to look out of the window. When things go badly they look in the mirror. In my experience most leaders do the exact opposite: when things go well they take as much of the credit as they can, and when things don't go well they look for someone to blame.

A DEPRESSING PICTURE OR AN OPPORTUNITY FOR REAL CHANGE?

So this is the state of the Stone Age company. It's a picture of ineffective leadership and dysfunctional behavior. It's a picture of money being made, customers being served, products being invented, all in spite of the management, not because of them.

It is a depressing picture, all the more so as the flaws are so blatant, and much of what I talk about in this book is frustratingly familiar to people who work in companies. We know it, we experience it, we learn about it in management schools, and read about it in books. And yet the status quo continues. Why is this? Can it ever change? If it can, how do we do it?

I believe change is possible. I believe that many people who are working in Stone Age companies are crying out for things to be different. There is so much to play for. If we want to create sustainable companies, then we should learn what the enlightened companies do and foster their values. Organizations would then become the places they should be: vibrant, inspiring, energizing, and creative.

In the rest of this book I look at what can be changed, how we can challenge the status quo, and I look at a new breed of leaders who are reinventing the way companies are run.

2

New frontiers: Why they need to change

WHAT'S THE BIG DEAL?

Talk to anyone running a company today, and chances are they would tell you that things are pretty much fine as they are. They would probably talk about the ongoing challenges of the market, the need to control costs, and their efforts to be more innovative and thus stay ahead of the competition. These things roll off senior executives' tongues. They operate under the implicit assumption that these are the problems that all companies must focus on.

They are on the defensive. They are defending themselves against external threats (the competition, the market, problems with customers and suppliers) and internal inadequacies (people not performing as they want them to, costs too high, lack of innovation, wasted time on politics, and so on). It doesn't occur to them to look at their business in a completely different way.

If they thought about how they wanted things to be and moved toward that instead of away from what they *didn't* want that would be a good start. You get what you focus on, and bosses focus on what they don't want.

LONG-TERM INVESTMENT

Companies have survived doing what they are doing in the ways that they are doing them for a long time. When I talked to people about this book and my belief that companies need to change, many of them challenged that. The majority of companies are, to a

---

TABLE 2.1 WHAT BOSSES FOCUS ON,
AND WHAT THEY SHOULD FOCUS ON

What they focus on	*What they should focus on*
■ Correcting people's weaknesses	■ Making the most of their talents
■ Cost cutting	■ Increasing revenues
■ Benchmarking the competition	■ Doing what their customers really want in the way they want
■ Setting narrow objects and putting constraints on people	■ Giving people more responsibility and holding them to their commitments
■ Eliminating failure	■ Using failure as a learning opportunity
■ Looking for what's wrong	■ Amplifying what's right
■ Carefully spun corporate messages to staff	■ Just telling them what's going on
■ Fuelling office politics by rewarding those who play that way	■ Rewarding openness and integrity
■ Short-term results	■ Long-term investment

---

greater or lesser extent, successful, so why would they need to change? However, I wonder how much more successful they could be if they were managed differently. And how much more pleasant and productive the work environments could be too.

Not questioning or even reviewing the status quo with an open mind is dangerous. However, the majority of senior managers don't question it at all. In the 1990s British Airways recognized the dangers of believing its own rhetoric, and took an unusual step to stop itself from doing that. BA appointed someone in the role of Court Jester. This person was the one who could say what needed to be said and what others were unlikely to say. I'm not saying that companies need to appoint such a person, but they do need to start to question their own assumptions, and managers inside them need to challenge themselves and their intentions.

At this point you might be saying, "Get real, this is all very well in practice, but in the real world companies could never change that much." My contention is that they can—and some already operate in very different ways from the norm. I show in Chapter 5 how there are some world-beating companies out there which are run very differently—and very successfully.

These companies have got it right and are sprinting ahead of their competition. And the competition do not realize that they have to add something to their list of things they have to compete against. It's not just technology, speed to market, innovation, or service—it's the very way the company is managed. This is the only thing that companies will be able to compete on in the future. Everything else is either too easy to copy or is dependent on the way the company is managed.

I am arguing that a new way of managing companies is urgently needed. It's not a nice-to-have. It is a matter of survival.

OPPORTUNITIES FOR CHANGE

The people who are running companies are obviously the ones who can change them if they choose to. Outside events can also create the possibility for change. Every so often something comes along that has the potential to change things in a big way.

Look at the dot.com boom of the 1990s. It was heralded as something that would change businesses' relationships with customers, change the business models, and would create a need for a very different kind of employee. All companies were affected in one way or another. Some completely reinvented themselves; others made small steps into the world of Internet business. Some of them installed sofas, coffee bars, and pinball machines to signify to others that they were taking on the dot.com culture.

Such symbols of trendy, up-to-date companies may have attracted some different kinds of workers, but they didn't change the fabric of the traditionally run enterprises. If anything, those companies now pat themselves on the back, relieved that they didn't succumb to dot.com fever. For sure, it's a good thing as many companies that staked their future on it are now out of business. There is a downside too, though. And that is that the people that run those companies are even more resistant to change, because in the 1990s they proved to themselves that it was a dangerous thing. They are never going to go there again!

In 2003 a series of events took place that was very effective in creating a certain kind of change in the corporate world. A number of scandals, the most spectacular of which was Enron, led to a scrutiny of corporate governance. Fear can create big change quickly. In this case it did. The change came, though, not in the values of the people who were being asked to run organizations, but in the form of regulation. This is typical of the way that people who run organizations react to a threat. They put in rules and processes to patch things up. Many corporations now employ CROs—chief risk officers. It says a lot about the mentality of a CEO who would create a job of chief risk officer but doesn't have a chief innovation officer or chief creativity officer.

Rules, regulations, and CROs don't solve the underlying problem. They only serve as a policing function. The root problems cannot be resolved with a rulebook. Fraud in corporations can never be prevented with regulations. There will always be someone clever enough to work his way around the rules. The only way to be sure that that won't happen is to hire people who would never do anything fraudulent. If all companies were run by people who had high integrity, they would hire people who had similar values. That is a much more effective way of protecting shareholders' interests.

The people who work in a company take their cue from the CEO and other leaders. If they are open and have high integrity, that sets the standard for everyone else in the company. WL Gore is best known for its GORE-TEX® fabrics but it also makes fluoropolymer products, components for the electronics industry, and medical products. All of its products are distinguished in their markets. It employs around 6,000 people in 45 locations around the world and its annual revenues top $1.5 billion. WL Gore looks for people who fit the culture. For instance, it doesn't want people who are concerned with status and power because that would upset the corporate culture. It filters out those people whose values don't fit.

We have seen some companies, and Enron was one of them, that talk about values and emblazon them on the walls for all to see. Paradoxically it is the companies that don't talk about values but just live them for which they are genuine. You can always tell whether companies are genuine or not about their values when they are tested. A company might say that treating people with respect, fairness, and integrity is its core value, but when one of its top salespeople repeatedly stitches up his colleagues and generally behaves badly, he is allowed to get away with it. Companies that genuinely object to that sort of behavior would fire these people without hesitation. When a company spouts one thing and does another, or allows someone to get away with "breaking the rules" for whatever reason, then it has lost the opportunity to change.

All the small acts of hypocrisy, letting a few people get away with things that the majority wouldn't, saying one thing and doing another—all of these things create a culture of cynicism and mistrust.

AND IF COMPANIES DON'T CHANGE?

The force against change is the number of powerful people who want their companies to go on as they are. They have a personal interest in things staying the same.

It's fairly easy to predict the consequences of increasing mistrust and cynicism in companies. Perhaps we can learn a lesson from the way it is in British and US politics. The electorate has become mistrustful of politicians. People are more savvy, and are becoming immune to the spin that politicians churn out these days. Unless a leader who people trust and believe, someone like Nelson Mandela, comes along, there is little hope for change. It's all too ingrained, and George W. Bush's and Tony Blair's intransigence doesn't open up any possibility for change. They are too driven by ego and power.

It becomes dangerous when we accept things as they are and can't imagine that change would be possible. It is getting to the point where we accept that that is the way that companies are.

It would perhaps be dramatizing to say that if the corporate world doesn't take a long, hard look at itself and change its ways, Enron-type scandals will become more and more common. But one thing is for sure. If companies could become less dysfunctional, such catastrophes would be less likely.

Let's play it out. Let's look at what can (and does happen) in organizations, and how that can lead to failure and ultimately their downfall. It seems simplistic, but these things aren't as complex as perhaps we like to imagine. Nor is fixing them—but that's for another chapter.

Imagine a company. It is in the finance sector, but in terms of the way it is run, it is very similar to lots of companies in lots of different sectors.

The chief executive (Bob) is very autocratic but in a gracious, gentlemanly way. He's a wolf in sheep's clothing, you might say. He has surrounded himself with people who are from very similar backgrounds and are highly intelligent. There are six of them. They are heads of business plus the finance director and the marketing director. Witnessing their executive meetings is fascinating. There is surprisingly little discussion. The CEO talks a lot and rarely asks opinions. It feels more like a series of lectures than a discussion amongst senior executives. Some of them are very ingratiating. The boss either doesn't notice or he likes it. Some bosses would find it extremely irritating.

I wonder what the shareholders would think if they could witness these meetings. If I were one of them I certainly wouldn't feel too comfortable putting my company in the hands of these people. They are running a complex, multi-million dollar organization, and yet they hardly ever disagree with each other, and none of them ever disagrees with the boss. What goes on in those meetings seems to be more about keeping the peace, not upsetting the boss, and keeping your head down as much as possible so as not to have it shot off. Since this CEO took over, the senior people have spent a lot of energy trying to impress him and taking as few risks as possible so that they don't make any mistakes. In short, it's all about the boss and not about necessarily doing the right thing for the company. He talks about "my strategy," and others talk about "Bob's strategy." It may seem like a small thing, but the language people use is significant. Talking about the strategy as "Bob's strategy" (which it is, as he hasn't involved or consulted anyone else) means that they feel no ownership. They may even feel no commitment to it.

Think about anything you do in your life. If it's what other people want, and they don't consult you and aren't even particularly interested in your opinion, how likely are you to put your heart and soul into it and really try to achieve it? It's common sense. So bosses like Bob who set the strategy and make all the decisions without consulting anyone won't be able to achieve as much, or as quickly, as bosses who involve people and gain their commitment by listening to them. Bob's way of doing things is predicated on the fact that he thinks he knows best. He's a very clever guy, but in the complex and ever changing world of business no one can know everything. Few talented people will put up with working for a boss like Bob who, quite frankly, shows no respect for them and doesn't value their contribution.

So what are the consequences for people in a company run by someone like Bob? They can be many and varied. Here are some of the things that happen:

- They start to take fewer risks.
- They second-guess the boss and only do what they assume he will approve of.
- They hide mistakes.
- They become demotivated.
- Their loyalty diminishes.
- They agree with the boss even if they know he is wrong.
- They stop bringing new ideas.
- They expend a lot of energy complaining to colleagues.
- They may even complain to customers.
- They take time off work.

- They spend their time on activities that will please the boss instead of on things that will please the customer.
- They stop thinking for themselves and just do what they are told.
- Some people take any opportunity they can to undermine the boss and damage his reputation to get their own back.
- If they are very different from the boss they become very stressed trying to become more like him or her.
- They start looking for another job.

All this adds up to a work environment devoid of trust, where people feel stifled and oppressed and not free to use their talent. It doesn't take a genius to work out how that can affect business. When people are so worried about pleasing the boss and terrified of upsetting him or her, that is what they are focusing on. They are not focusing on their clients.

Some people in these environments become more and more like the boss. They start to act like him or her. They don't do it consciously and are unaware of it. Then there are the other types of people who have a strong sense of themselves and remain themselves despite those around them. Predictably, life is much harder for these people. They either get more stick from the boss, or they have to pretend to be a certain way in front of him or her. For both types of people it is very stressful, because they are on edge and expending a lot of emotional energy (consciously or unconsciously) being something they are not, or at the very least, molding themselves into a shape that is not natural for them.

Now we can see how high the cost is of appointing such a boss. (I won't use the word "leader" as people have to want to follow a leader. People only follow this person in order to survive.) There is a cost to the health, well-being, commitment, motivation, and loyalty of the workforce. There is a cost to the customer, who takes second place. Creativity and innovation are destroyed because people dare not take risks, and you cannot have innovation without risk. The organization's ability to attract the best people suffers greatly, because really good people want enough freedom to decide for themselves what to do and how to do it. The reputation of the company suffers because people talk—to their families, friends, and customers. In short, the company becomes stifled and restricted. A company run by a dictator is never as successful in the long term for all these reasons.

WHAT ABOUT THE SHAREHOLDERS?

Senior people in companies talk a lot about the shareholders. Financial results are measured in terms of "total shareholder return." If you listened to the talk in the executive suite you could be forgiven for thinking that these people are really committed to providing the best return for shareholders. Let's check this out. How many people in companies do you know who do what they do with shareholders in mind all the time? Hopefully they have customers in mind all the time, but shareholders are mostly a passive group of people and/or set of companies who we can't characterize and often don't know. It's hard to feel committed to something that feels so abstract.

However, CEOs clearly have to keep shareholders in mind, deliver a satisfactory return for them, and make sure that they are confident in the company's ability to deliver what it says it is going to deliver. But is shareholder value really the thing that motivates the CEO above all? Of course it's not. After all, the CEO is only human. We sometimes forget that. But she is susceptible to the same failings and insecurities as the rest of us. The thing that really motivates the CEO is securing her position (in the company and business community as well as financially). Part of the job is to make sure the shareholders are happy enough, and to mingle with the important, large shareholders to make sure they have a warm, comfortable feeling about the person in whose hands they may have put lots of their money. CEOs know how to do this. Amazingly, they are hardly ever challenged by shareholders even when things go wrong. The place where you may hear shareholder's concerns and challenges is at company AGMs. I have never heard a shareholder ask any particularly tough questions at AGMs. I can understand why employee shareholders wouldn't, but I can't understand why the others wouldn't. It seems incredible that having invested their cash in a company, they are prepared to accept what they read in the annual report and what they hear the CEO say at the annual AGM, and not probe it any deeper.

So we see another force against change in companies. Shareholders have a lot of power because they have the money. Yet they are incredibly passive, and are mostly unaware of what needs changing so that their invest-ments are protected and, what is more, have a better chance of growing.

I recently changed banks. I had been with my bank for 20 years and had had reasonably good service. That was until something went wrong, and the way the bank handled it was a catalogue of disasters. Good customer service did not feature, even when I wrote and complained to the CEO. I have now changed banks but I have also sold my shares in the bank. I have totally lost confidence in its ability to protect my investment. It is losing customers in droves to a competitor bank whose service is, in my experience so far, personal, caring, and they do what they say they will do.

CUSTOMERS—THE REAL HOPE FOR CHANGE?

If shareholders are unlikely to influence companies to change, maybe customers will. They are the ones to whom companies should listen. Individually maybe they don't have the influence, but collectively they certainly do. And for business-to-business companies all it takes is one or two big customers to demand change, and it's a dumb company that doesn't listen. They have a lot of clout.

Until recently customers' concerns centered mainly on the products and services that they were buying—quality, cost, and the service they received. Nowadays they are showing an interest in the leadership team, the environmental policy, how socially responsible the company is, and what sort of a company it is to work for. Some are even starting to wonder about values, and want to do business with companies whose values they support. An extreme example of this is consultancies who won't do business with tobacco companies or companies that make weapons.

THE INVESTMENT COMMUNITY AS CATALYST FOR CHANGE

The investment community too—that paragon of institutional conservatism—is also a potential catalyst for change. Investors are looking at more than just the hard numbers when they are making investment decisions. They are realizing that the leadership team and the company culture have a huge amount to do with its success, and they are increasingly adding such factors to their list of criteria for investment decisions.

COMPANIES CAN'T GO ON LIKE THIS

It is easy to identify the enormous forces that keep our companies the way they are, even when it is startlingly obvious that they need to change. However, forces are building that are gradually starting to topple the increasingly wobbly foundations of the Stone Age company.

There are the combined pressures of customers not only demanding a better service, but also becoming more interested in the ethics of business, as well as investors looking at the so-called "softer" side of how business is run. These pressures can only get stronger. Companies need to start responding to these pressures, or they will increasingly lose business to ones that customers feel good about doing business with.

3

The urge to retreat— what stops companies changing?

Companies desperately need to change. The business world is awash with change consultants and coaches. If change weren't necessary, CEOs wouldn't spend the amount of money that they spend on all those consultants. It's a million-dollar industry. Yet nothing much seems to change. Some of the work that is going on creates short-term change but it doesn't last.

WHY DON'T COMPANIES CHANGE?

There are three core reasons: they don't want to change, there are too many people who are invested in the company not changing, and they are addicted to the hierarchical system of management. They don't know how to create the change they need to make. No one has figured out a way that works, and even if they did know how to change there is not yet enough pressure to change from customers, shareholders, or investors.

WE'RE COMFORTABLE AS WE ARE

It is not just the people at the top of the tree, those with power, who don't want to change. Despite the fact that many people complain about and laugh at their bosses, many of them don't want things to change either. There is a certain comfort in the system of hierarchy. We can blame those at the top, as well as handing over all responsibility to them when things go wrong. There is something about human beings that makes them want to locate those above them and those below them in the pecking order. And part of organizational life for many people is complaining about those above them and trying to gain power over those below them. In less hierarchical, or democratic, organizations a lot of energy is put into making sure that people don't slip back into the hierarchical way of acting and thinking.

We are so used to things being organized in a hierarchical system that it is very natural for us. The family is a hierarchy, with the parents being in charge, one of them being the supreme leader. School is a hierarchy, with the head teacher at the top in overall charge, and power distributed to deputy heads, heads of department, and so on down. The further down you go, the less power you have. The children, of course, in families and schools are at the bottom. So it is ingrained in us from an early age that that is how things work. Few of us ever question this, and we expect it to continue into adulthood. Indeed, most organizational systems that we encounter throughout our lives are hierarchical ones: the military, the church, educational establishments, and our workplaces.

We are comfortable with hierarchy; we consciously or unconsciously find our own place in the various hierarchical systems that we belong to in our lives. We may be at the top of the family hierarchy, further down the work hierarchy, and towards the top of the tree in a club that we belong to away from work. It is easier for us to accept hierarchy than to challenge it. Fear as well as comfort plays a part. Challenging the authority of a "superior" is a frightening thing to do, as we may suffer reprisals. So, we can see that hierarchy is a sturdy system that is held in place by two of the most powerful psychological drivers in human nature—safety and fear.

Hierarchy is not all bad. Its advantage, apart from the fact that it is so familiar and comfortable, is that it is clear and easy for people to understand and relate to. You could also argue that it keeps things orderly and avoids chaos. However, in today's complex and fast-changing world, the disadvantages of hierarchy outweigh the advantages. Companies structured along hierarchical lines can't learn and change because people spend their time doing what those above them tell them to do. If they can't learn they can't adapt. So unless the person at the top learns something new and is prepared to adapt, nothing will change.

For power-hungry people who like to order others around, hierarchy supports their self-image. Without it they would feel like nobodies, because their self-worth is built around their position. Herein lies another major flaw in hierarchy. These types of people are attracted to and fit well into hierarchies. They spend much of their energy bolstering their positions and pleasing those above them. Their priority is to maintain their position and achieve their personal ambitions. Their need for power and status far outweighs their commitment to a cause bigger than themselves.

HIERARCHY—THE BIG BLOCK

There are usually, and thankfully, many other types of people who keep a company running well. These are the people who get on with the job, work with those they need to work with to get the job done, and don't get sucked in to power relationships and politics. They are part of an informal network inside the company. They follow the rules, of course, but their prime focus is doing the job.

The hierarchy is the thing that imposes many unnecessary rules, systems, procedures, and meetings. It is not the thing that makes the company efficient and allows things to get done. It is often a huge energy drain and distraction. People spend time producing endless reports, measuring things that can't really be measured, and answering questions from those above them instead of getting on with the work that makes a difference. One of the arguments that proponents of hierarchy put forward in its favor is that it is needed to make sure that task allocation is done efficiently. It is of course important that people know what they are responsible for, and things get done without too much duplication, but a hierarchy isn't the only way to achieve this. In fact I show in Chapter 5 that some companies have found much more effective, and motivating, ways of doing this.

Any organization could survive without its hierarchy, but no organization could survive without its prevailing culture, values, and the people who work within it. It is all of these things combined that give work meaning for people. It is these things that make people decide whether they want to work for a company. The hierarchical structure is not something that motivates people to want to join a company, although it is often the reason for people leaving.

It is interesting to look at how things actually get done in a company: that is, the network versus the hierarchy. All companies have an informal network of people who are connected and help each other. It is these networks that provide the impetus and motivation for action. They also provide the support and allegiance that most of us need if we are to find our work enjoyable and rewarding. In many cases the network compensates for the lack of a boss's support or input. People still engage with the hierarchy out of necessity, but the real work gets done outside of that.

NETWORKS—THE KEY TO CHANGE

A group creates its own culture, and what you find in reality in companies are a number of different sub-cultures that coexist within the main company culture. Bosses are often oblivious to how things really get done, and how much "working round the system" has to happen. They really don't understand the power of the networks. In fact, it is important that they continue to ignore the networks. The minute they start paying attention to them, they would cease to be informal networks, they would get dragged into the hierarchical system, and all the benefits of them would be lost.

If, somehow the power of these networks could be harnessed and there were a few influential people supporting them, companies would stand a chance of changing. If enough people were "recruited" into the culture of the network, then gradually the way they did things would become the norm, and quietly accepted. A mistake that companies make over and over is to bring in "change initiatives." The first flaw in that approach is that quite often the people who bring them in are not clear (or convinced) about whatever change they want to bring about. The second flaw is that common sense is always ignored. People won't support change unless they really want to. They may have to play the game and pay lip service to change initiatives, but they will never wholeheartedly get behind them. And wholeheartedly getting behind something is the only way of making it work.

The majority of books about organizational change fail to acknowledge the real way that people and organizations work. They use the hierarchy as their framework for designing the change program. This approach is clearly flawed in that it ignores the fact that the informal is a hugely powerful influence on how things really work. The dilemma is that ignoring it means that change will never have a chance of working, and engaging with it makes it part of the formal structure of the company, so the positive effects of change are dampened.

"DOING TO" VERSUS "ENGAGING WITH"

Another major mistake that people miss about making change is that you can't "do it" to people or groups of people. Actually they can't even "do it" to themselves.

Organizational change programs don't take adequate account of how people are able (or not) to change. It is a complex process. First of all people have to really want to change. Even if they want to, actually changing is not as easy as it sounds, and won't automatically follow. I have witnessed many people in their lives trying to change in a certain direction. Even when they *really want to* and have a lot of support and help, it is often so hard to change. Sheer willpower doesn't do it. There is no formula, and it is certainly not a cause and effect process. The truth is that there are many things that can cause a person or system to change. Some have instant effects, some may take a longer time. It is a highly complex process that we tend to over-simplify.

MBA courses cover organizational change in one module, and typically take a very rational and simplistic view of it. Of course you have to simplify in order to understand, and so that you can actually take action on things without being overwhelmed by the complexity of them. However, companies treat organizational change as if it is a fixed destination, and they choose one route. Because bosses are typically not too open to trying new things out, living with ambiguity, and changing their minds, they spend their time getting people to measure things, and convince themselves that what they are doing is making a difference. They will almost do anything other than admit that they might have been wrong, or something didn't work as well as it should have done.

It is rare that executives will be open to anyone telling them that they may have got it wrong and it would be a good idea to take another look. It would mean so much to employees and do so much to build trust and loyalty if they could do that. It's so simple but they just don't get it. So many senior people are highly internally referenced, and would not even consider that someone else might be right, or that they might have got something wrong. Being right is very important to them. It is much more important than building a culture of trust where people can freely challenge and admit to mistakes. Some of them really do think that they are right all the time, whereas some of them secretly know they may not be, but consider that it may be showing weakness to admit to that.

BOSSES ONLY HEAR WHAT THEY WANT TO HEAR

Few bosses want people around them who really challenge them. Few are emotionally secure enough to take it. Even when they know that they may be wrong, they feel that they can't back down, whatever the cost. Many of them go around kidding themselves that all is well in their company. You only have to go to management conferences and hear what CEOs say about their companies, and compare it with what some of the workers in the company say, to know that. There are some companies that make it onto one of the many "Top 100 companies to work for," lists but you only have to talk to acquaintances who work at those companies to know that there is a mismatch between the "spin" and the reality. You may argue that it's OK for companies to talk themselves up to the outside world. It's just smart PR, right? The real worry, though, is when they try to do that internally, because everyone knows the truth. Most people are fairly savvy about what their company is really like, and can see right through the hype, but companies insist on doing it.

Here's an example of what one company did. It cost it

a lot of money. The company undertook an employee climate survey. Its stated purpose was to create more "employee engagement" by asking the staff their opinion and taking action on the areas of concern. The survey posed questions to gauge how much the staff knew about the company's strategy and policies, how good they felt communication was, what they thought of the training on offer, and so on. The real reasons for doing it were nothing at all to do with building employee engagement. Here are the real reasons. And, by the way, you could apply these very same reasons to many different initiatives that companies undertake:

- To make the HR director feel like she is doing something important.
- As a vehicle for some people to further their own agendas/promote their own hobby horses.
- To provide "evidence" to back up certain PR messages that the company wants to send.
- To enable the CEO to feel that his company is "up with the times" and that he doesn't feel left out when talking to peers in other companies.

Far from making the employees feel listened to and involved, the survey made them feel manipulated and angry. The issues that they really wanted the company to address, like pay and how they were managed, did not appear in the survey. The CEO had taken those questions out. The ones that he left in were not going to evoke any controversial answers. It was all very bland, and didn't give the CEO any news that he didn't want to hear.

Instead of resulting in the employees feeling more engaged, it made them cynical and angry. Companies should only do climate surveys if they are prepared to ask the questions that need to be asked, and are prepared to listen to the answers. Otherwise they destroy any trust and confidence that exists.

IMAGINING SOMETHING DIFFERENT

I was recently at a seminar where someone from WL Gore was talking about his company and how it is managed. It is unconventional and very successful. The audience's reaction was as interesting to me as the story itself. Some people really struggled to see that what was being presented was a very different concept and framework for managing. Their questions were not set in the context of that framework; they were questions that applied to the only framework that they knew. It was hard for them to conceptualize anything other than how things are currently. This is what happens when people are stuck in a rut. Providing they have a sense that they want something to change, they first need to be able to imagine something different, even if they can only do that very vaguely. Even though senior managers sometimes invite people to challenge the way things are, they rarely mean it. And certainly to challenge the very way that organizations are set up would be a step too far.

The truth is that the majority of bosses in organizations do not really want anything to be different. They are personally and professionally invested in things staying exactly the same. They have built their careers around the hierarchical system. They have their power base, their status, and the perks that come with management. Unless they are pioneering types of people who are motivated by changing the system, there is absolutely no reason for them to do so, as there is no benefit to them. Of course the pioneers tend not to end up in other people's companies, they tend to run their own companies or work in creative or development-oriented environments where they do have freedom to change things.

So you see how difficult it is to create change when the people running companies don't have the predisposition or the motivation for it.

SO WHAT IS THEIR MOTIVATION?

Think of all the managers you know who want to do the right thing, who have the interests of the company at heart, for whom work is about leaving a legacy not about personal ambition. They listen because they really want to do things the best way possible. Can you think of many of those? I really tried hard and I can think of seven people, and I have probably known a couple of hundred managers altogether in my career so far.

Most senior managers are motivated by factors that are not that positive, and hinder rather than help. Not all of these factors necessarily result in something bad. These managers have to have a positive intention. They have to have the best interests of the customer and the shareholder at heart. It's when they mainly have their own interests and furthering their own careers at heart that things start to go wrong. I am not saying that good managers are totally altruistic. No one is. We all do whatever we do to meet our own psychological needs. Even those who dedicate their lives to helping others are ultimately doing it to make themselves feel good. Maybe they get a sense of self-worth from it, or they get approval from others. This isn't bad. It's just how we are as human beings. What makes it bad is when managers do the things they do with the intention of gaining for themselves irrespective of whether or not it helps the company or the people in it. Most of these managers want the company to do well, of course, because that makes them look good. But they make decisions based on how they will help them, not necessarily on what is the right thing to do. Here's how these people are motivated:

- Having power over others.
- Being right.
- Winning (and others losing, not win–win).
- Furthering their own careers.

I stress that it's not about just being nice or altruistic. Table 3.1 has profiles of two very successful, but very different, senior managers. Have a look at the differences.

These two are both successful in terms of business results. The one on the left, however is not trusted, has little or no loyalty from his staff, and does not create an enjoyable workplace. The other guy is well respected, has an army of loyal staff, and believes that you can achieve a lot more if people are happy and having fun.

TABLE 3.1 TWO MANAGERIAL STYLES

Mr 'I'll get what I want'	Mr 'I'll make a difference'
■ He is autocratic (he thinks he knows best)	■ He provides vision and involves people. He knows he doesn't have all the answers.
■ He likes to have power over people because his ego needs it	■ He likes power because he can use it in a positive way
■ Failure is not acceptable	■ He believes that failure's inevitable sometimes. The important thing is learning from it.
■ He's not a people person	■ He believes that it's the people that make business happen. His job is to lead them, inspire them, and help them to succeed.
■ Everything has to be perfect	■ His approach is "get on with it and improve it as we go along"
■ The most important thing is his career	■ The most important things are the customers, his people, and making a difference
■ He sucks up to the people above him and stamps on the ones below	■ He works with the people who can make things happen, whoever they are
■ He is a master at politics (and loves it)	■ He accepts politics exists but prefers not to engage with it
■ People are afraid of him and hide mistakes	■ People go to him for help when they make mistakes

He knows what's going on because people are open with him, talk to him, and aren't afraid to tell him when things are going wrong. The first one is the so-called "hero-CEO" type. He gets short-term results. The second one is the type needed for long-term success.

In a nutshell, the first guy is the reason that companies can't change, and the second guy provides the hope that they will.

HOW DO INTELLIGENT PEOPLE LET IT HAPPEN?

This picture is probably very familiar to you. Amazingly, the autocratic leader survives and thrives amongst even the most intelligent followers. I have seen young managers promoted, and change to become the most objectionable and autocratic leaders possible. People who were once their colleagues become subservient and afraid. The other day I had a conversation with a friend of mine, a manager I respect greatly. He is a real asset to his company. He is creative, very committed, and loyal. He was relating the tale of his new boss, a much younger guy who had been promoted to the position and was really throwing his weight around. My friend told me that he was scared of him.

I was amazed at this. How could such a capable and successful manager be scared of this chap who seemed like he didn't even deserve much respect? It was simple. He has the power to fire my friend if he gets on the wrong side of him or doesn't play the game, so my friend is allowing himself to be held hostage to this man. Don't get me wrong, I can understand why. He has a family to support and bills to pay. He has been in the company a long time, and feels that he doesn't have many options. Besides, he loves the company and his job, and doesn't see why he should be pushed out by this guy. However, he knows that unless he plays the game in the way his new boss wants it to be played, he will be out.

SELLING OURSELVES OUT

I don't blame my friend for how he has chosen to respond to this boss. It is understandable. He is a clever guy and has dealt with bad bosses before. I have no doubt that he can do it again. But he is selling himself out. He is giving up on his own principles. He is compromising himself and is behaving in ways that are not too comfortable for him. Like all bullies, bosses like this can only get away with it because the people that work for them don't protest, and because the people above them let them get away with it. We are all complicit in the system. It is not easy to step outside of it and protest, especially if you are the lone voice.

That is why many people allow themselves to be treated badly. They choose job security and a quiet life over being true to themselves. The irony is, though, that their jobs are never secure. They are living under the illusion that if they toe the line they will be OK. But anyone who has ever worked for such a boss knows that it is never OK. It is like living with an abusive parent or husband; there are periods of calm where they are happy and not picking on you, but you always know that at some point it will start again. The price of putting up with it is high, and it is constant.

An organization is a system. And a system can't be sustained unless the players in it act and react in the same way. Employees acting the way my friend did towards his boss perpetuate the system. The boss's boss (in Bob's case this is the chairman of the company), by allowing him to get away with this behavior, is also perpetuating the system.

I recently got chatting with someone on a train. She regaled me with her story of her job at a law firm where she had worked for several years. It was a tale of bad treatment and bullying. I couldn't believe that she had put up with it for so long. It seemed to me like she was her own worst enemy, particularly as she had expertise that was in great demand. Eventually she was forced to leave because she had a nervous breakdown. That was 18 months ago. She is now fully recovered and working in a job that she loves for a boss she thinks is fantastic. I asked her why she stayed in the awful firm for so long, and why she let herself be treated that way.

She said she did it because she was scared that she wouldn't get another job, and scared that if she was offered one, she might get a bad reference from her boss. Fear held her back. She was her own worst enemy. Despite the fact that she knew she was very marketable, she was too afraid to take the risk of leaving. You can bet your bottom dollar that others will be working in that firm putting up with the same sort of treatment as she did.

HOW DO WE COPE?

The lawyer in the story above clearly didn't cope very well, and it took a serious illness to change things for her. Hopefully cases like this are rare. However, if we believe what we read in the media, cases of mistreatment of employees are becoming increasingly common these days.

Thankfully, the majority of people don't have nervous breakdowns as a result of having awful bosses, although some most certainly experience stress and other psychological ailments. People who find themselves in a similar position to my friend have to find strategies to cope with the situation which help them to minimize the stress. Some are compliant and change themselves to fit with how the boss wants them to be. Others protest openly and find themselves in constant conflict with the boss (that is, if they get to keep their job for long enough!). Then there are the type of people who are compliant enough to make their work lives bearable, but resist passively where they can. They manage to find a way of living with themselves and maintaining their professional and personal pride, while keeping the boss happy enough that life is bearable. Then there are the types that vote with their feet and leave.

WHEREFORE ART THOU, HR?

It is a commonly held fallacy that if you have a problem with your boss you can go to HR and they will help. Most HR people have no interest in getting involved with these tricky issues for which there are no clear-cut rules. They have little or no knowledge of how organizations work or what drives people psychologically. Most focus on policy and policing, and the majority haven't got the courage to stand up to badly behaved bosses. HR directors rarely have an interest in organizational dynamics, let alone the understanding to spot what is really going wrong, and the capability or guts to do anything about it. The answer definitely does not lie within the walls of HR.

If HR are the guardians of people policies, then what are they up to if they are not addressing the badly behaved people in the organization? The answer is that they are concentrating on other things, and hoping that the really tough people problems will go away. The best-case scenario is that they might suggest "coaching." Now I happen to believe that coaching can be a powerful and effective way of creating change. However, for it to work it has to be predicated on a number of things. The most important of all these is that the person is capable of changing and actually wants to change.

Here's a classic case of where coaching was used when actually the person should have been fired. Sadly this type of case is not unusual. For many years this man had been a pain to work with. He was a sales guy. He would steal other's leads, undercut the prices that his colleagues had quoted to customers, terrorize his staff, and generally be an extremely difficult person to work with. So much time was spent mopping up after him, mediating when he had got into scraps with colleagues from other departments, and generally smoothing the effects of his bad behavior. He was out of control. Why didn't his boss try and stop him? The answer is that he brought in the money, and the company was afraid that revenues would drop without him. It was being held to ransom. The clever people who were running the company couldn't see that they could undoubtedly hire a much better salesperson, who was also a good sales manager and didn't cause trouble wherever he went. Instead they opted for keeping this man on and putting up with his destructive behavior. So everything else the company was doing to try and get people to live by a certain set of values and behave in a certain way to each other lost all credibility, not to mention the high staff turnover (and cost of that) because people couldn't stand working for him. In a nutshell, all trust had broken down.

Eventually, the CEO insisted that his manager confront him about his behavior and that he be given help to improve. When the manager talked to the sales guy and told him that he really needed to change, it was like speaking to him in a foreign language. Of course he understood what the manager was saying, but it was so far away from how he knew how to be that he couldn't envisage how to be different. It was like explaining to a fish that it needed to get out of the water and start breathing the air outside. He really couldn't get it. Not only was it unfair to put all the other people through what they had had to go through for years with him, it was also unfair to try to force him to change into something that he really couldn't change into. However, not to be thwarted in their mammoth efforts to keep this guy employed at all costs, the company did what many had done before it and no doubt what many will do again. It hired a coach for him.

Many a coach has been hired to fix issues that weak managers have not been able to fix. What beats me is that coaches worth their salt would take on such a job. I believe that a vital part of what qualifies someone to be a coach is his high level of integrity. Maybe I am being unfair. Maybe the coach in this instance genuinely did feel help could be given. You would have thought, though, that given the history of this salesman, the coach would have realized it was unlikely that the person was going to change. The big missing ingredient was that he didn't want to change. And if someone doesn't want to, you can't make him or her do so.

The really important thing about this story isn't to do with the bad employee who senior management didn't deal with. The really significant thing is the messages that this sent to the entire company. Everyone knew of this man, of course. Such stories travel fast. All the good work that the company was doing to promote collaboration and fair treatment was undermined. HR and senior managers close their eyes to this. They don't want to hear it. They don't want to hear it because all the employee climate surveys, competencies, performance management and so on—all of it loses credibility. You can't lose credibility a bit, it's all or nothing. So, for the sake of not dealing with really bad behavior in just one guy, they lose the respect and trust of everyone else.

Of course employees will play the game, but deep down they know where they stand. And deep down their loyalty is damaged. There is only one exception to this, and that is if people elsewhere in the company have a boss to whom they feel personal loyalty. That personal loyalty can replace the lack of loyalty to the company as a whole. It is still damaging, of course, because the company has built up little factions of people whose loyalty and support remain but become precarious, because if their boss leaves, it's gone.

WHAT VALUE LOYALTY?

Companies try to achieve loyalty. It's a valuable thing. If people are loyal they are committed, they are good ambassadors and they stick around. You can get away with paying people a little less and getting them to work a little more if they are loyal. It's a valuable asset to have. The word "loyalty" isn't used so much, probably because it's very difficult to define and even more difficult for most bosses to figure out what to do to gain it. It's a bit like trust. The paradox is that the more you try to achieve it, the more elusive it becomes. Those who talk about trust and loyalty are less likely to inspire it than those who just act in ways that create it (usually without knowing that that is what they are doing because it is so natural to them).

THE FORCE FOR CHANGE VERSUS THE SEDUCTION OF THE STATUS QUO

Whatever aspects of life we look at, we can see that human beings often opt for what they have now, rather than venture into the unknown. Few people really relish change. Even those who do have to call upon a great deal of courage in order to step away from the familiar and towards uncertainty.

So it is the case in companies. Year after year they stay with the tried and tested. They may take baby steps into new ventures and new ways of doing things, but for the most part change is incremental and organic, not radical or conscious. The cost of getting it wrong is simply too high for most CEOs. And the obsession with measurement, justification, and logic is a defense against dealing with the reality. The reality is that markets, customers, and organizations are complex, unpredictable, and ambiguous. Most senior executives prefer to believe that, if they only they put the right measures in, they will be in control.

So we can see how inertia wins, and why, in this age where we have a huge amount of knowledge about what works and doesn't work in organizations, we have yet to find the wisdom to do what we know works.

4

Not up to the job— why bosses don't deserve to be

"Why does she do it? We just don't understand." This is something that people say the world over about their bosses.

Egotistical, egomaniac, mean, bullying: these are such common accusations about bosses. We've already had some examples of autocratic bosses. It's clear that this style is the least effective way of motivating and managing a company. However, it is still the favored approach of many bosses.

In this chapter I am going to take a look at why it is that these people still have most of the power in companies today, and why this is the critical factor that needs to change.

WHO'S THE CEO?

It is received wisdom that the CEO is the main determinant of a company's culture. The effect of the CEO can't be reduced to a cause–effect equation, but certain things happen, or not, depending on what type of person he is. Let's have a look at a couple of CEOs.

Rhonda is the CEO of a large international company. She is straight-talking, has a clear vision of what she wants, she takes risks, and she is commercially astute. So far, so good. The problem with Rhonda is she makes bad hiring decisions. She is not a good judge of people. She tends to hire people who amuse her, rather than people who are competent. She doesn't realize that this is what she is doing. She kids herself that they are good at the job too. Actually, it is worse than that. She can't really be bothered to spend a great deal of time and effort hiring people. She finds it a bit dull and boring. So a great many unsuitable types have been waved through the door! One senior person that she hired told me that when she turned up for the interview, a very rushed Rhonda greeted her with "Hi Angela, I've lost your CV. Come in and tell me about yourself. I've heard you're great!"

Rhonda is also a control freak (like many CEOs). She spends her time doing things you wouldn't expect a CEO to spend time on, such as writing copy for some of the marketing material (and she is no marketeer).

Rhonda has a lot going for her. But what we are look-ing at here is the effect that her personality and style has on the way the company works. She is such a strong personality (and has surrounded herself with much weaker ones) that there is no one who will question her judgment on anything. As a result she has made a few bad decisions, including an acquisition that went wrong. Since that happened many of the senior people in the company frequently discuss why it was a bad decision, and say that she should never have gone ahead with it. None of them, however, opposed her at the time. Because she has a dictatorial style people shy away from challenging her, and distance themselves from those decisions she takes that they disagree with.

So we can see here how the style of the top person can affect the success, or otherwise, of a company. If she had not made that acquisition the company would not have lost the shareholders millions of pounds. With Rhonda, though, there is no way that she wouldn't have made that decision. She was determined and she didn't listen to others. Even if she hired strong people capable of challenging her, they would end up fighting all the time or they would leave because they wouldn't be able to cope with her autocratic style.

You might classify Rhonda as a command and control type of leader.

Here's an example of a different type, a control and consensus type. It sounds like a contradiction in terms. However there are some leaders who are like this. I have met a couple of them. It can be very confusing for the people who work for them. If Rhonda incites rage in people, this type incites profound frustration. Here's a profile of this type of leader, based on a real person. John runs a large international company. He has high needs for control, just like Rhonda, and pretty much every other CEO in the world. He is very difficult to read, he isn't good at building relationships, and deep down he is insecure about his own ability to do the job. He appears to be charming and gracious but there's a real dark side. The executives he appoints are domineering and bullying characters. It's almost as though he likes to have henchmen to do the dirty work that he is too weak to do himself. He is unlikely to be aware that that is what he does. He obviously has lots of power, being the boss, but it is as if he is afraid of exercising it directly. He doesn't expressly give power to others, but allows the ones who want to take it to do what they want with it.

There are some managers in the company who are incredibly badly behaved, and John doesn't step in to stop it. If it's a really bad situation, such as one that could result in litigation, he will say something to the person concerned, but only if really pressed to do so, and not in a very direct way. And on the rare occasion that he does intervene, it is not in a commanding way. He "suggests" courses of action to people, so if they don't want to do what he says, they don't. His messages are unclear and coded. So for him to say to someone, "I don't expect the status quo to prevail," means, "There's a part of this situation that you really ought to change, but I will leave it up to you to decide." You can see where the frustration comes in.

John is also not a decision maker. All decisions have to be reached by consensus. He simply will not say, "This is what we are going to do." He certainly won't step in and sort out disagreements and arguments between the senior executives. People rarely agree, of course, so hours are taken up debating issues, and wasting much time trying to come to a decision. In the end things are watered down and fudged in order that the majority can buy in. This makes for mediocrity, and certainly doesn't support creativity and innovation.

People have little respect for John or the management decision-making process. They often can't be bothered to put forward new business ideas because it takes such stamina just to go through the whole consensus-building process. The ideas that do get through are always very low risk, low cost, and therefore are never going to result in substantial growth. Nor are managers likely to hugely motivate or excite those who are working on them.

There are no shared values in either Rhonda or John's management teams. Both of them just bumble along fairly passively. Most of Rhonda's team haven't got the courage to challenge her and create real debate. Most of John's team reluctantly spend hours trying to build consensus, occasionally looking to John for some strong direction, never finding it, and getting frustrated along the way. In both cases it means results that are not as good as they could be. In Rhonda's case it is first, because she is not good at choosing the right people, and second, because she thinks she knows best, so she makes all the decisions. In John's case it is because no one is ever going to take a decision that sets the world on fire because of the need to consult everyone and get their support before it happens.

The bullies in John's company are free to behave towards their staff as they wish. This is bad in itself, but what is worse is that John espouses fairness and employee respect while allowing the bad behavior to continue. There are a few people who have pointed out to John how these people behave, some in very strong terms. His answer is to bring in a coach to give them an assessment and development plan. Guess what? Some of them get a coach. It never makes any difference.

HOW DO THEY GET TO THE TOP?

There are obviously many varieties of people who become senior managers. There are however certain characteristics that they share. Someone once said that psychopaths and CEOs are very similar personality types. They are narcissistic (the world revolves around them), they have a higher than normal need for control, many of them are socially inadequate in some way, and they have a low need to give or receive affection and a low need to be included.

Considering these traits, it starts to become clearer how it is possible for these people to get to the top of the organization. There are other factors too. Here's the kind of things that they typically do to get on:

- They network with the right people at the right time.
- They suck up to those more powerful and influential than them.
- They put a lot of energy into managing their image and reputation.
- They do what the boss wants (which is not necessarily the right thing).
- They adapt their focus to gain favor from whoever is their boss at any one time.
- They become a person that the boss wants to be around —whether that means clever, amusing, a gossip, a pseudo-challenger, a yes-person, or whatever.
- They read the boss well so that they know what to do to please her.
- They do some good pieces of work that the boss can cite as reasons that they are the ones to be promoted.
- They spend most of their time looking towards the top of the organization and not at their customers or their staff.
- They have the ability to sniff out others with power and influence over the boss, and align themselves with them.

- They are single-minded in their objective. No one will stand in their way.
- They are cold and rational, with not much of the human touch.
- They are autocratic and uncaring to their staff, unless being otherwise will somehow further their career.
- They have an internal locus of control. In other words they are not influenced by others' views or opinions (unless of course a particular person could have some influence over their career).
- They are not open to being challenged or to learning to do things differently.
- They are very good at politics.

Few of these characteristics are those that make for a very effective leader. As David Whyte, the poet, said, "Good leaders treat other people as if they are alive, not as though they are bit players in their career drama."

THE OTHER PIECE OF THE PUZZLE

There is one piece of this puzzle missing. It is a crucial piece, and has to do with the leader's intentions. Simply put, this is the one thing that differentiates the best leaders from the others. Good and strong leaders have the interests of the customers, shareholders, and staff at heart at all times. These are the things they focus on. Some people spend their time on this; the others spend their time on managing their own careers and their own ambitions. If headhunters weeded out the latter, the quality of the CEOs managing today's companies would go up markedly. Obviously all of this is presupposing that they are also technically competent in whatever field they are in. Given that they are, leadership ability is the thing that makes them great leaders and differentiates their companies from the less successful ones.

So why don't headhunters weed the less good leaders out? Quite simply it's because the qualities they have are the ones that are valued. This is the model of "leadership" that has existed for years. Even though there are masses of research and hundreds of courses at business schools on how to be a good leader, the current style and wisdom prevail.

ALL THE RESEARCH AND BUSINESS SCHOOL COURSES HAVE MADE NO DIFFERENCE

The reason for this is that CEOs are not really interested in changing themselves or the status quo in their companies. Why would CEOs be interested in research that tells them that what they are doing doesn't help make their companies effective? They are hard-wired not to be open to learning and doing things differently.

The lack of ability to learn is a major problem for companies today. If you have the capability and willingness to learn, then you have the ability to change. Change won't happen if people can't learn.

It seems to follow that the higher up people go in companies, the more closed they are to learning. Perhaps it is because they feel as though they should know everything they need to know, and admitting they don't makes them feel incompetent and vulnerable. I was once having a conversation with a senior manager about his development. He said he thought he didn't need any. Apart from doing the kind of courses where you acquire more knowledge, he is not evolving as a leader at all. He really thinks he is perfect as he is. There is no humility, just arrogance. I find it frightening that people with that attitude run organizations. They not only stop themselves learning and evolving, they get in the way of others doing so. Companies run by people like that become soulless and stale. Thankfully there are usually people who are so oriented towards improvement and learning new things that there is some energy that creates change despite how the bosses are.

"I'M THE BOSS, I'VE GOT NOTHING TO LEARN"

Bosses who are not prepared to admit that they have something to learn and are not willing to change if necessary are negligent. Here's a real-life example to illustrate why this is true and how serious the consequences can be.

Harry was a senior executive. He was competent at what he did. He kept the company efficient, mainly through cost control. He avoided any difficult issues to do with people. He never gave any feedback (positive or negative). He just couldn't bring himself to do it. He attended a leadership development program at one of the European business schools. It was aimed at very senior executives and it was heavyweight. Delegates' staff and colleagues had been asked to give feedback on the participants anonymously before the program. This was passed on to individuals concerned in a personal session with a coach. The coaches also observed the participants in a number of exercises and gave feedback based on their own observations.

Harry was told that he was uninspiring as a leader. He didn't have a clear vision and he certainly didn't display any passion for anything. And people didn't feel motivated by him because he never praised them when they were doing well, and he didn't give them guidance when they were going wrong. Some of the people who worked for him were pretty angry, because they felt that they had been given some veiled messages from Harry, but he had never been straight with them. One person said he thought Harry wanted him out.

For some reason Harry found it very difficult to have real conversations with people. Harry's conversations were veiled and coded, and if he could, he would use others to convey messages. The result was that people spent their time second-guessing Harry, and they did not feel at all motivated by him. Nearly all of them said they felt short-changed. In terms of the effect on the business, there were the obvious issues of people feeling demotivated, which results in lower productivity, and a couple of them said they were looking for other jobs because they were imagining that Harry didn't want them there. That may or may not have been true, but they were "reading between the lines," and that was the conclusion they came to.

Harry understood the feedback, but he really saw no need to change. His view was a very rational one: "They are grown-ups, they shouldn't need me to tell them whether they are doing a good job or not." Irrespective of seniority, everyone needs praise and feedback. It just wasn't in Harry to do it. I suspect that he had never experienced it himself when he was growing up as a child, so he had no model of how it might work. He also confessed that he hated to get close to people. Having personal conversations with them, whether about good or bad stuff, was excruciatingly uncomfortable for him. Again, he had never had that experience himself in his life, and just didn't know how to give it to others.

This lack of ability and lack of willingness to learn to do things differently almost cost him his job and the company millions. Sue, the HR director, came to him one day because someone had approached her and told her that a senior director had been bullying her for years and that she couldn't take it any more. Sue had heard stories about this person's behavior before. She was very concerned about the woman, and worried that she might take some kind of legal action against the company.

Sue talked it through with Harry and explained the legal position as well as her feelings about the moral position. Harry said he already knew about this, but "What could he do about it?" The bully in question was a crucial member of the management team and had the power to sabotage the company if challenged. Harry was scared of him.

Sue realized that the only chance she had of getting Harry to take action was to scare him about the potential legal consequences, so she brought in a particularly hard-talking lawyer to discuss the case. The lawyer was clear. If Harry didn't formally warn the person concerned that he had to stop this or he would be fired, and the woman who complained then took legal action (which she could on several counts), the company would lose the case hands down. Not only could it cost a lot of money, it would certainly be damaging to the reputation of the company. Harry would clearly have to go too. The court would look very dimly on him, because he knew about the man's behaviour and had not been prepared to do anything to stop it.

This was extremely serious. Harry squirmed and tried every angle to avoid and delay. He tried to get Sue and the lawyer to talk to the manager concerned. He just didn't want to face it himself. He never had that conversation, even though there was a huge amount at stake: his job, the health of an employee, a potentially nasty and expensive lawsuit, and his company's reputation. It was astonishing.

Harry got away with it on that occasion, as the person who had complained left a few months later. The person who was being bullied told Sue that she felt totally unsupported by the company that she had worked at for 20 years. Her husband wanted her to file a lawsuit against the company, but she said she couldn't put herself through the stress of that. So Harry got away scot-free.

Senior people like Harry don't deserve to be in the jobs they are in, and companies like his simply don't deserve to survive. He could go on hundreds of courses, have hours of coaching, and it would all be a waste of the company's money. He just does not want to change.

WILLINGNESS TO LEARN—THE MISSING LINK

People who are arrogant and egotistical don't think they need to learn anything or do anything differently. As we saw from the tale of Harry, this can be a very dangerous strategy. The world's, the market's, and the customers' demands change so fast these days that learning and adaptation are essential commodities for companies. It's incredible that so many of them are in denial about this.

The problem starts in schools. We are not taught to learn in schools, we are taught how to find the right answer. Learning is about being adaptable, about seeing what needs to change; it's about experimentation and being open. The experience in most companies is also more about getting it right than about learning. People are expected to find the right answer and not to make mistakes.

The exception is companies that have to invent or create new things. I spent some time working with an innovation consultancy when the company I was working for at the time was starting to get demands from customers to come up with "never been done before" ideas. It gave us an interesting insight into how stuck we were in our ways. We did some idea-generating sessions. We had ground rules including "Don't knock, build." This was incredibly difficult for some people. Their whole "training" had been to critique and find what was wrong with things, not to support people and help them to build their ideas.

This is how senior managers are. It is almost as though they don't think they are doing their job unless they are able to spot what's wrong. This is particularly prevalent in the British culture, where we tend to focus on the negative and what's wrong with something, rather than what is working about something and the possibilities. Paying attention to what's wrong has the effect over time of decreasing options and possibilities. It does not lead to the expansive thinking that most CEOs would probably say they wanted.

WHO GETS TO BE MANAGERS?

The people who make it to the top of the tree are just like the ones who are already there. They learn how they need to be if they want to get to the top. And the people at the top hire in their own image. Ability to do the job is the least important factor. Learning the rules of the game is the most important one. Ironically it is usually the people others least want to follow who end up becoming promoted. Think about the people who have become managers. How many of them are really good at managing and motivating people? How many of them really want to be managers? There is usually an inverse relationship between the capability to be a manager and the likelihood of promotion.

There are a few different types of managers.

Petty tyrants

These are people who have been given a little bit of power and use it over others to make themselves feel important. They spend their time figuring out how to please the boss and sucking up. They like the control they have over others, and spend the rest of their time ordering their staff around. Their peers don't respect them because they see how these people behave totally differently around them depending on their importance in the eyes of the petty tyrant. Petty tyrants are usually not the most talented in their jobs—they have got on not through ability but through ingratiating themselves to the boss.

Petty tyrants are insecure people whose identities depend on their own sense of how important they are. They are the types no one really likes or respects. Their staff feel unsupported by them, because they spend their time criticizing and controlling and not helping them very much. Their peers spend time with them only if they have to. They realize that petty tyrants have their own agendas, and only bother with them to the extent that they can be useful to them. Peers don't particularly respect their professional knowledge and expertise. Nor do peers rate their abilities as managers, because they have heard so many stories about the way they manage. Peers know that these people tend to have very high staff turnover in their department, and get very annoyed that no one questions them on it. Petty tyrants only get away with it because they are in with the boss and "play the game."

The reluctant ones

These are the people who are very good at their job and so have been put in charge of others. This happens so often in companies. There are many people in management positions who really don't want to manage staff. They know they are no good at it but they do it because it's a promotion and it is sort of expected. It is a mistake to put these people in management positions. It causes both them and their staff stress. You would have thought that companies would have learnt by now that this is not a good idea. It is rare for people to turn down promotion to become managers. They accept it because they feel they should; that it would be a black mark against them if they didn't say yes to the job. Only rarely do people realize that becoming a manager would not make them happy, nor would it serve the company well.

I have only ever come across one person like that. He was an excellent salesman—one of the best I have ever met. He has spent the previous ten years resisting promotion. The two companies that he had worked for in that time were extremely impressed with his performance, and kept trying to persuade him to become a sales manager. They assumed that because he was excellent at his job (and was a great role model for other sales people), he would also be excellent at managing a sales team. Luckily, for everyone concerned, this chap knew what he loved doing. He loved selling. He didn't love managing other people. He was not seduced by the idea of an executive compensation package and higher status. He was one of those rare people with enough self-awareness to know that the job as a manager would not suit him, and enough self-confidence to say no.

The ones who really want to be managers but aren't up to the job

The third type who should never be managers are those who really want to be managers, try really hard to get it right, but aren't up to the job. These are the type of people who go on the courses, read up on what they should do, but just can't translate the theory to practice and haven't got the credibility. These types do everything by the book; appraisals are done on time, they have regular meetings with their staff, send them on training courses, and do all the things that the books say a good manager should do. However, they don't inspire people, they don't have a vision, and are not great communicators. These types aren't disliked. There is nothing really to dislike about them—they are trying hard to do a good job. But they are just fairly ineffectual.

The irony is that the people who get to be managers are the people who others least want to follow.

OVER-MANAGED AND UNDER-LED

Managers perceive their jobs to be to control and monitor people's activities. Even businesses that provide "intelligent" services such as consultancies and law firms are run along old-fashioned lines. They have a hierarchy with several levels of management each monitoring the level below. The reasoning behind this system has long since faded, and companies don't think about whether it's the best way any more. The "intelligent" workers of today who are talented, self-motivated, and know more about their field of professional expertise than their managers do, don't need managing in the traditional sense. They may need support, help with tackling organizational issues that get in their way and so on, but they don't need to be controlled. It is laughable that the ineffectual types of people I describe above actually end up managing them.

A friend of mine is an extremely talented marketing executive. She runs her own geographical region and is highly respected by all of her colleagues. The global marketing job was up for grabs recently. She didn't get it. One of her peers did. He got it rather than her for a number of reasons. He is close to the corporate headquarters (she isn't), and he had spent the previous 12 months positioning himself for the job by getting close to the CEO, taking credit for work that the global team had done, and generally acting as if he was the boss already. In the meantime, my friend got on with the job and handled the tricky global projects that he didn't want to and, frankly, wasn't up to anyway. He had no interest in doing the real work. Like many people who make it to the top, he was more interested in advancing his own career, and spent his time doing as much self-promotion as possible.

My friend is now in the position where this guy does her appraisal and tells her what her weaknesses are (because he's the type of person who doesn't talk about people's strengths—that is far too threatening to him). She is far more competent and committed to her job than he is. He relies on her to make sure that things are done right. Yet he will never acknowledge this. Without her he simply wouldn't be able to sustain his position. And he only has her on the team because she was there already. All the others that he has hired are fairly weak because he is not the kind of person who would hire anyone good who might challenge him.

It is galling to my friend to have to answer to someone like this who she has no respect for, who doesn't appreciate her, and uses what she does to further his own position. She finds it even more annoying that he has the power to make judgments about her performance and pay.

This sort of scenario is not uncommon in companies. There are thousands of people like my friend who are propping up incompetent managers and allowing the system to continue.

WHY DO WE PUT UP WITH IT?

My friend puts up with it because she loves her job and the people she works with. She has decided that it's worth it for that. But her boss does nothing to help her or motivate her. Many people complain about their bosses and feel as though they hinder rather than help. Imagine how much more motivating and productive people would be if they had bosses who made their lives easier instead of harder. The fact that it seems like an impossible dream says a lot about the state that we have allowed businesses to get into and now accept as inevitable. The companies that are doing it differently are really in a position of huge competitive advantage.

Homer Simpson had a comment to make about the cost of bad leadership. "If adults don't like their jobs they don't go on strike. They just go in every day and do it really half-assed."

A whole company full of people doing it "half-assed" is a big cost to carry!

IT DOESN'T WORK ANY MORE

The system of hierarchy and management is outdated. It is tied into the post-industrial model of organizations. The notion of management is predicated on the belief that people can't be trusted and won't work unless they are monitored and controlled. What managers spend their time doing is organizing other people, doing their appraisals, checking up on them, reporting their collective activities to their own bosses, doing various reports and administrative tasks for HR and so on. All this costs companies huge amounts of money and time. It is simply not the most effective way of getting the job done well these days, yet few companies question it, and even fewer do it differently. There is hope; there are some companies that do things differently, and we look at them and how they do it in Chapter 5.

There are good reasons that we don't question the whole hierarchical management set-up. If we did, it would be those with the power and the perks who would lose. It simply won't happen in established companies unless a few enlightened CEOs come along. But, let's face it: enlightened CEOs who are likely to change the status quo are unlikely to be appointed.

THERE IS HOPE

People are starting to challenge the "command and control" style of leadership. A lot more is being written about it, and the syllabuses of business schools are full of courses on "enlightened" leadership. Jim Collins's book *Good to Great* is a bestseller. Jim talks about what he calls "Level 1 leadership." These leaders are the ones who "look in the mirror when things go wrong and out of the window when things go right." They are very different to the types of bosses that I have described in this chapter.

In the various "Best companies to work for" listings that the *Financial Times*, *Fortune* magazine, and others compile, one of the criteria is always the leadership. The belief that good leadership is values-based is becoming more and more common. Even government is starting to acknowledge that a different way of running companies is needed. Why else would Tony Blair have invited Richard Reed of the Innocent drink company to speak to government about how he runs his company?

In the Western world of business people are becoming more concerned about ethics. Sure there is a lot of talk about corporate social responsibility, but it doesn't mean much. Many companies pay lip service to it and do whatever they do because they feel they have to, as well as for PR reasons. But there are those who really do care about people and the role of business in society, and are calling for a more responsible way of managing businesses.

It may take some time, but the companies I have talked about in this book who run in outmoded ways will eventually be forced to change, or be squeezed out by a different breed of company run by a very different breed of boss. The groundswell against the Stone Age company and Stone Age bosses is now such that they won't be able to sustain their current ways.

My advice to all the managers out there is, change or you'll soon be defunct.

5

Enlightened or radical? The companies of the future

So far it has been a bleak picture. Stone Age companies are run by people who have lots of power but not much integrity. Old-fashioned ways of managing don't work in the modern world. And good employees stay committed and motivated in spite of the management, not because of them.

Few of these companies will change because the people who run them don't want them to. Over time they will lose ground to those organizations that are doing things very differently. Some will see the writing on the wall and try to institute radical change. They may make it in time or they may not. Others won't even notice the threat and will die gradually or suddenly. There is an urgent demand for companies to be different, and they are not noticing it.

THE COMPANIES OF TODAY

There are companies operating very successfully right now that are run in new ways. They are companies of our time. There are relatively few of them but they exist. And they are successful. They are in all sectors, too. You may imagine that the intelligent industries like consulting and IT would be the likeliest candidates for forward thinking and innovative management. It's not so.

There are some businesses in decidedly unglamorous fields that are overturning everything we thought about how to run a business. They are challenging the assumptions we didn't even know we had. There is SOL, a cleaning business in Scandinavia; Semco, a Brazilian manufacturing company; WL Gore; Ritz-Carlton, and

Southwest Airlines in the United States. They are being heralded as the ones that have got it right. Some of their people do the speaking circuit, and they are inundated with companies that want to have a look at what they are doing and learn from them.

These companies don't have a formula that they all follow. They are all very different, and each has its own essence and feel to it.

THE ENGINE NOT THE POLISH

These companies are enlightened. The paradox is that they don't think of themselves that way. When I heard Bob Doak of WL Gore speak about his company, the thing that astonished me more than anything he said about it was that he didn't seem to realize what an amazing company WL Gore was. It reminded me of when I spoke to someone at WWF (the World Wildlife Fund) about trust. She told me that it hadn't occurred to her until she spoke to me that her organization had a trust-based culture. It was just part of the values that everyone that worked there held, so much so that they were not conscious of it.

I am not saying that WL Gore doesn't deliberately try to create a company that works well and is as healthy as possible in every sense of the word. But WL Gore is so clear about what's important and its company values that it can't not create what it creates. It's an expression of what it is. It is not a means to an end. That's the mistake made by other companies that try to emulate companies such as WL Gore. It doesn't work.

The majority of companies that are trying to change won't manage it because they are focusing on the wrong things. They are not looking at their values and what they really care about. They are trying to copy "good working practices." It doesn't work. It's like polishing a car—it may look immaculate but if the engine is wrecked it is no good.

There's a great story about Bill Hewlett of Hewlett-Packard. One day he found the door to the supplies room locked. He cut the lock off with bolt cutters and left a note saying, "Don't ever lock this door again." The message was that Bill trusted people. Most companies say they trust their staff but lock their supplies cupboards. These companies say one thing and do another. The truly great leaders don't rely on words because their actions speak so much louder. They focus on the engine not the polish.

A FAIRYTALE FOR OUR TIME

Once upon a time there lived a man and his wife. They had both worked for many years in a factory near their small town in the United States. In the evenings over dinner they would often talk about work. These were not the usual conversations that most men and their wives have about what this person or that person has done, or what pay rise they think they will get, and how their boss treated them that day. They talked about why things were as they were at work. They talked about what work meant to them and what they thought it meant to the bosses and employees at their factory. They had so many questions, so few answers, and so much of what they experienced made little sense.

After a while their evening-time conversations gradually turned to how they would do things if they ran their own company. They got very excited about this and would talk about it for hours on end, in lots and lots of detail. If we were there, reader, we would be urging them to do it, so compelling was the picture they painted, and so excited were they about the possibilities they talked of.

After a while, they had talked and dreamed about it so much that one night the man looked at his wife and said, "Let's do it." She was stunned for a moment. How could it not have occurred to them sooner that they should do it, she thought?

People who are motivated by a passion and who operate with integrity are the greatest leaders. This story of a man and wife creating a vision of a new breed of company could have been the tale of the beginnings of WL Gore.

WL Gore is known to be a highly innovative company. It is distinguished by its culture. Bill Gore started the company in 1958 when he left Du Pont where he had worked as an engineer for 17 years. He was a real pioneer. It is unusual for leaders in 2005 to realize that hierarchy doesn't make for innovation. Bill Gore realized this and acted on it almost 50 years ago. He created a culture that was, and still is, very different to that of most companies. He did it because to him it made total sense, and it was a practical, effective, and humane way of running a company.

The company is thriving today and is still thought of as radical in the way it is run. If you look at how it works it all makes total sense. And it certainly turns over our assumptions of how companies need to be managed. It is a frightening reflection on our times, our outdated views, and our arrogance, that WL Gore is so far from the norm.

WL Gore's objective is "to make money and have fun." It believes that everyone is in the same boat and need to support each other to meet the commitments they make to the company and their colleagues. WL Gore subscribes to four principles:

■ Fairness
  – to each other
  – to suppliers
  – to customers
■ Freedom
  – to help others with their commitments
  – to make a bigger contribution
■ Commitment
  – each person makes their own commitment in their field
■ Waterline
  – they think of the company as a ship and don't take any decisions that might hole the ship.

There is no chain of command at WL Gore. This is challenging at times. Some people drift towards making rules and creating hierarchy. Trust is key to this way of operating. People do not take the view that trust has to be earned, they presume that trust exists. If someone breaks the trust the company will be patient, but if it happens again the person has to leave the company.

There is no chain of command but there are leaders. WL Gore says of the leaders, "Look over your shoulder to make sure someone is following you." The leaders of projects are decision makers but they do not have power because of their status or position. They have power because they have expertise and the other people in the team trust and respect them and want to follow them. The firm sees leadership as a bank account—if people respect and trust you, you earn the right to make withdrawals. I wonder how many managers in other companies even have a bank account that is in credit, let alone have very much in it.

Bill Gore understood something fundamental about people and communication way back when he set up his company. He understood that you need to keep groups relatively small for them to be effective. This principle is as true today as it was in the 1950s. The company keeps work units down to below 150. Everyone must know everyone else by name. Groups of people form around projects. They are close-knit teams and each person in the team makes his own commitment to the team and the project.

The leader usually emerges. If one doesn't then the team hires one. At WL Gore leadership is about having the influence, expertise, willingness, and commitment to want to lead a particular team in a certain pursuit. Leaders get to be leaders because they are chosen by their followers and they choose to take the job. In ordinary companies leaders usually do it because it's a way of getting up the ladder, not because they are committed to doing it.

Think of something that you really want to do and are committed to. Now think of something that you do because it's a means to an end and you feel you have to. Notice the difference in energy between the two. The leadership horsepower that exists in WL Gore is massive compared with that of others companies simply because the willingness is there.

The way that WL Gore decides who gets paid what fits totally with the culture of commitment and responsibility too. Compensation is based on contribution. The members of each team rank each other according to what they each feel each other's contribution is. There is inevitably disagreement at times, which is handled through having sensitive but honest conversations. Mostly people feel that it is a fair system. It is certainly not secretive, as it is in most organizations. And it is not the bosses on high deciding what people should get. Managers tend to know less about what people do and how they do it than their peers do. At WL Gore people are accountable, and it is clear to their colleagues what they are, or are not, contributing.

WL Gore is also unusual in the way it relates to its customers and suppliers. It talks to customers about what they need. Many companies claim to do this, but what they actually do is mold what they have to make it look like something that fits what the customer wants. Or in the words of a salesman I talked to about this, "I know where I want to lead the customer, and I just have to ask him the questions that get me to that point." This is manipulation, and any smart customer will see right through it.

WL Gore focuses on value, not cost. The company view is that if what it is offering is something that the customer really wants, if it is valuable to him or her, then both parties gain.

However, it is not Utopia. And it can be stretching for people because it is so different from what they have been used to. Some of us are programmed to strive for status and position, and we naturally look to see who is above us and who is below us in the pecking order. I spoke to someone who joined WL Gore from another manufacturing company. In his previous company, his job title was vice-president. It gave him status; everyone knew how important he was. He said that he struggled to suddenly be no more important than anyone else and to have a business card with the word "associate" on it. (Everyone is called "associate.") People from outside the company ask him what he does, and struggle with not being able to place him in a hierarchy. WL Gore wants to hire people for whom the work is of primary importance, not their status. At WL Gore there is no hierarchy. It calls this a "lattice" organization.

The bottom line is that life at WL Gore is about taking responsibility, making commitments, and teamwork. People who are motivated by these things do well. There are types who wouldn't work there or, if they did, would struggle with it. They are the people who need the status and power that go with having a certain position in a company. Status and power at WL Gore comes from being valued and respected for who you are and what you do. It takes secure and confident people to be able to work in an environment like this.

WL Gore is very successful because it is innovative, efficient in the way it works, and cares about relationships with customers and suppliers. It doesn't divert from its principles. WL Gore is clear about what it cares about and is 100 percent committed to whatever it decides to do. It is not half-hearted and it doesn't pay lip service. Everything it does has to be valuable, and it doesn't do "me too." WL Gore doesn't give up and it refuses to stick to rules and conventions that don't make sense.

The company is known for breaking down conservative and restrictive industry norms. It had tried for years to get consumer products manufacturers interested in its technology for producing a superior dental floss. It had no luck and lots of resistance. In the early 1990s the company took matters into its own hands and took Glide to market itself. WL Gore built a demand by giving out free samples to dentists and hygienists. It was one of the earliest examples of viral marketing.

The company did the same with Elixir guitar strings. The product was expensive at $15 each—more than three times the price of other strings. Retailers wouldn't stock them. The team at WL Gore was so convinced that once guitarists realized how much better the product was they would want it. The company gave away 20,000 samples to subscribers to guitar magazines. It was a success. Elixir now leads the market with a 35 percent share.

CAN IT BE COPIED?

The systems and way of working in WL Gore are easy to copy. Senior managers from well-known companies rush to seminars to learn what they can and take bits and pieces back to their own companies. They leave what they perceive to be the difficult stuff (like pay) and pick up some of the more symbolic things (like no job titles). Of course that makes absolutely no difference. The *whole system* has to be in synch. And at the root of what makes the difference, and what makes WL Gore such a success, is values. Success at WL Gore is about much more than profit. It is about creating a place of work that is fun, inspiring, and rewarding too. The company takes it seriously and sticks relentlessly to its principles. It doesn't make exceptions for so-called rainmakers, and that is the big mistake that other companies make.

Changing today's companies is not a matter of starting initiatives, setting up new processes, and rearranging boxes and arrows. It is a matter of creating workspaces where people can find meaning and feel some passion about what they do. All significant achievements need energy, passion, and momentum. Most companies today have a strong intellectual and empirical capacity. Those things are important but they are not the ingredients for the companies of the future.

When companies have a strong values base, the culture that flows from that is alive and vibrant with possibility, because people can find meaning. Simply put, they know what the organization stands for and have decided that they personally can buy into it too.

It is like having a higher purpose. When people work with a higher purpose in mind, the commitment and spirit are evident. When they don't, it is an effort of will to get things done, rather than something that resembles a calling.

WHO ELSE CAN WE LEARN FROM?

Timberland—doing well and doing good

. Arguably the world's best example of a values-led organization, Timberland is not only hugely successful but is also a caring corporation. Corporate social responsibility means something at Timberland. It affects its relationships with customers, suppliers, distributors, and employees. The way it engages people and animates the brand is world class.

Timberland was founded in Boston, Massachusetts in 1918 by Nathan Swartz. Nathan's grandson now runs the company and has turned it into a genuine, and rare, pioneer of socially responsible corporations.

Timberland's *raison d'etre* is to make quality products and to make a difference—"to our jobs, our lives, and our world." Timberland says it "invests in the communities where we live and work and do our best to do good by:

- Offering the consumer a company to believe in and get involved with.
- Offering our employees a set of beliefs they can stand behind.
- Offering the community help and support at all times.
- Offering shareholders a company people want to buy from and enjoy working for."

Timberland is another example of a company that has been operating for years and that still has the values of its founder at heart. It is privately held and so isn't beholden to external demands from the investment community and shareholders.

SOL—the cleaning company with a heart

Any company can have values regardless of what type of company it is and which sector it is in. Any company can be a good place to work as well as being commercially successful and great with customers. SOL is a Scandinavian cleaning company. Its business is office cleaning. People are organized in self-managed teams. They decide upon their own objectives and agree their budgets. They have the freedom to do whatever they feel they need to do to make their customers happy. They don't have to check back with their bosses. They are trusted. The CEO trusts them to do what they say they are going to do. She says that they usually set much higher standards for themselves than she would set for them.

Southwest Airlines—a world's best

For years Southwest Airlines has been cited as one of the world's best organizations. It is regarded as the world's most customer-oriented, profitable, and innovative airline. It's mission is "dedication to the highest quality of customer service delivered with a sense of warmth, friendliness, individual pride and company spirit."

Directly after September 11, employees at Southwest volunteered to give up some of their pay to keep the airline profitable. I can't imagine workers in many other companies doing that. It goes some way to explaining why its market capitalization was greater than that of all the other US airlines combined.

The author Kevin Freiburg said this in his and Jackie Freiburg's book, *Nuts!: Southwest Airlines' crazy recipe for business and personal success*: "The more we saw people search for meaning in their work, the more we wanted to share the principles behind Southwest Airline's success. With most people we shared with they felt uplifted, inspired, and challenged."

The reasons for Southwest's success, aside from its sound business model, are basically the same as the reasons for other enlightened companies. Southwest trusts people, treats them with respect (not as "resources"), celebrates the good, learns from mistakes, and makes information available to everyone. None of these things are overlooked in deference to policy or procedure, as is the case in Stone Age companies.

Wegmans Food Markets—winning hearts and minds

Wegmans is one of the largest private companies in the United States. It was founded in 1915 as a family business. Again, strong values about how people should be treated and how customers should be served underpin the success of Wegmans.

It is the number one company to work for on the *Fortune* 2005 list. Its story is an extraordinary one of outstanding service delivery. The way it does this is by showing its total commitment to employees and customers. It's a big company, and with 34,000 employees that is a real feat. Such is its appeal that in 2004 over 2,000 customers wrote to Wegmans asking the company to open a store in their neighborhood.

Wegmans raised the bar on the shopping experience with better quality goods, a huge range of goods, beautiful stores, and astonishingly high levels of customer service. Wegmans is an early adopter of new technology that enhances the customer experience.

The company believes it is ahead of the game because of the people who work there and the principles they follow. Again, it's back to values. The company's values are borne out by its community and charitable work as well as the way it treats employees. The company has won dozens of awards and distinctions for making the shopping experience better, and for treating customers, employees, and communities well.

Richer—in more ways than one

Richer Sounds is a successful UK hi-fi chain. Its founder, Julian Richer, has developed a rewarding and trust-based culture, so much so that he has lists of people wanting to work there. One of his key principles is that the sales staff take responsibility for doing what they think is appropriate to make the customer happy. To enable staff to do that confidently there is an in-depth training program that covers product knowledge, building relationships, how to handle a range of tough situations, and more. New hires have a buddy so that they have someone to help, support, and guide them in their first few months. At WL Gore everyone is called an "associate"; at

Richer Sounds, everyone is a "colleague." Julian Richer insists on this out of respect for his people. Everyone has a contribution to make, and there is no benefit in differentiating people by job title. Like Bill Gore, Julian Richer established a framework, based on values that set out the rules of engagement. Within the framework people have the freedom to do what they need to do.

Semco—democracy in action

Semco is a Brazilian manufacturing company. It is uncommon in the way it is run. Although it has a hierarchy it is run on democratic principles. In his book *Maverick* (1993, Arrow Books), Ricardo Semler, the CEO, says; "We have absolute trust in our employees, in fact we are partners with them."

In some of its practices some would certainly say that Semco is radical. When Semler suggested to his top managers that they allow the staff to set their own pay, they thought he had gone crazy. They couldn't imagine how costs wouldn't go spiraling up as people gave themselves ridiculously high pay rises. Semler asked his secretary what she thought. She had a very different view. She thought that people would be fair about it and pay themselves what they felt they were worth. Semco introduced the new system and it works. People set their pay according to a number of criteria: their value to the company, what they think they could earn elsewhere, how much colleagues with similar responsibilities make, what their friends make, and how much they need to live. When they introduced this system Semler and his team were surprised how often people set their pay lower than the managers would have done.

Semco is another great example of how when we really examine the assumptions that underpin what we find, we are unsure of what those assumptions are because we have never thought about them. Or if we have thought about them, they are very often flawed.

In the case of how companies approach pay, there are many unchallenged rules and assumptions. There is also a fundamental lack of understanding of how human beings work. There is also an unwillingness to change the way things are done. That can be laziness, it can be a lack of ability to think in innovative ways. Semler was committed to creating the best business that he could. He is a pioneer, a lateral thinker, and a creative man. As we know, these are uncommon traits in a leader.

Orange—courage and creativity

I love Orange. My love for it has come from being a customer and having some great experiences. These are experiences that I talk about a lot and experiences the like of which I haven't had with any other companies. The experiences include losing my phone and getting a new one couriered the next day to a place in the country where I was staying. The one that stands out the most, though, and that I love to tell people, was when I took my mum into an Orange store to talk to the staff about whether she should go from pay-as-you-go to a contract phone. She wasn't even on the Orange network but having experienced great service from the company when I had recently upgraded my phone, I felt sure that its assistants would do what they could to help. I was right. The guy in the store advised her on that, suggested that I give her my old handset, and transferred the sim card for us. As he was doing that, mum mentioned to me that she was thinking about getting a case for the phone. He turned and picked one off the display and handed it to her—free of charge. Orange got no business from my mum that day, but it got several customers afterwards as a result of both of us telling many people about our experience.

To the rest of us, the enlightened companies are courageous. They take steps that Stone Age companies would simply be too cautious to take. Take Orange's radical step to remove sales people from its phone shops. Customer feedback told the company that people hated going into phone shops. Their overriding dread was dealing with the phone contracts and the paperwork involved. So Orange decided to do something that would help its customers as well as take the pressure off them. Orange made all its sales staff into trainers instead. They were no longer incentivized on how much they sold but on how many customers they trained, *whether or not* the customers bought anything.

In the first few weeks sales dropped. Most companies would probably stop the experiment at this point and go back to how they were. Orange had such belief that this was the right thing to do that it continued. Within three months footfall and sales had both risen substantially, and staff turnover had fallen.

The philosophy of Orange is that you have to put customers first. Commercial good sense sometimes stops that happening. As long as customers benefit and it makes sense commercially, Orange will do anything. So far it has worked. Orange certainly stands out above all other UK mobile phone companies. None of them can compete on technology, Orange decided to compete on service. The company now has a cool brand that customers feel good about.

To make its phone trainers initiative a success, it did a few small and simple things. Orange was careful not to over-complicate things, something that Stone Age companies can learn from. First, Orange paid incentives on numbers of customers trained, not on sales. The company trusted the sales people to record their numbers. Second, Orange trained them and gave them some guiding principles on how to treat customers. Third, the company told them how they would be measured.

Every month an undercover researcher would come into each store posing as a customer. The researcher would video the person who helped him or her. The entire team's bonus for that quarter would depend on how that person did. When this was first explained to the trainers, some of them complained that it was unfair that if one person did a bad job, they should all suffer. However, what in fact happened was that teamwork became excellent. The staff helped and coached each other, and when new staff came on board they made sure that person did a great job too, so that they would all get their bonuses. That simple step not only improved customer service, sales, and perception of the brand, it also resulted in high-performing and motivated teams. It made people want to stay, and created a demand for jobs in Orange stores.

If Stone Age companies were even to think of such an innovative idea, let alone try to implement it, they would be extremely concerned about managing risk and controlling the situation. They would probably take ages to decide whether to do it, they would water down the scheme to make it less risky but also less powerful, and they would put in complex monitoring systems. They wouldn't even think of changing the basis on which they rewarded their staff, because they would be terrified that sales would drop. Their focus on short-term results not long-term value would strangle the scheme before it started. And finally, because they wouldn't change what they rewarded people for, they would have to find a way of encouraging staff to want to train customers as opposed to sell to them. So guess what they would do? They would send them all on a training course, which would take ages to design and would probably make little difference, because training courses rarely do unless people have a good reason to apply what they learn. In short, they would still be thinking about it while Orange was stealing the march by just getting on and doing it.

WHAT DO THESE ENLIGHTENED COMPANIES HAVE IN COMMON?

- They have clear principles and values and they stick to them relentlessly.
- They don't do things because they always have. They do things that make sense to them and their customers.

- They are open-minded, they question their own assumptions, and encourage others to do the same.
- They want to learn. They encourage innovation and new ways of doing things.
- They are managed openly and without political agendas.
- People are rewarded according to their contribution, not on their status and position in the pecking order.
- The only legitimate use of power is the personal power that people earn because they are respected. It gives them influence.
- There is no place for ego. People are expected to do what they do because it is for the good of the customer and company, not because it furthers their own agenda.
- The atmosphere is positive and free of fear.
- People are encouraged to take risks and mistakes are viewed as opportunities to learn.

These characteristics can be true of any organization in any sector, whether it is a business, a school, a hospital, or a charity.

In these types of organization there is always a leader who embodies the principles. He is a leader who is clear about what's important and sticks to his beliefs. In the case of WL Gore it started with Bill Gore and his wife. They created the only company that they could create— one that fitted with their values and their strong beliefs about how people should be treated. WL Gore was, and still is, an absolute reflection of their values. The culture they created, the stories that are passed down from one generation to the next, are such that the culture continues. People are hired to work for WL Gore who believe in it too. It has become a virtuous circle

THRIVING VERSUS SURVIVING

At the heart of any organization are people and relationships. There are the employees, the managers, other stakeholders, customers, and suppliers. There are processes, regulations, and systems that make it all work too, but without the people and relationships nothing can happen.

People have become more demanding about what they want from work. It used to be that a wage and job security was all they could have hoped for or expected. Think of mine workers in the 1950s. They wanted enough money to feed and clothe their families and a safe work environment. By today's standards these were relatively low expectations. They didn't get paid enough, and when a miner was sick or died in a pit accident his family was flung into poverty. Thankfully these sorts of employment conditions are pretty rare in the western world today.

Today we want much more from our employers, and we think of our relationship with them as a two-way contract. Remember the phrase that was popular in the 1990s, the psychological contract? It implied that in return for our work, our commitment, and our loyalty, we would get good pay and conditions, fair treatment, respect, and meaningful work. Employers had a tick-box approach to this. Psychology didn't come into it. To most companies it is about proving their pay is in this or that quartile, that they have an equal opportunities policy, and that they have a discipline and grievance procedure.

Another piece of jargon that has been adopted by companies is "employee engagement." Most companies try to get it by doing the same sorts of things that they do to fulfill their side of the "psychological contracts." Many companies take it seriously. They realize that disengaged employees don't mean great business. In a *Gallup Management Journal* Employee Engagement Index survey (2004, Gallup Organization Research) of more than 1,000 US employees, 71 percent described themselves as either disengaged or actively disengaged from their work. I don't think this statistic is astonishing to most people who are working in corporate life right now.

Companies that have employees who are engaged, energetic, and full of passion for their work have a huge asset. They don't get employees to be like this because of some employee engagement initiative, it happens as a natural consequence of the company being as it is.

THE TRUTH ABOUT PASSION

I heard the poet David Whyte give a talk about leadership. He was saying that what corporations need from their people nowadays is flexibility, adaptability, creativity, and passion. He invited the audience to imagine a manager calling in a member of staff for a performance review. He told her that she scored 8.2 on adaptability and she really needed to be a 9.5 at least. Her creativity was too low as well, and he needed her to step it up from a 6 to at least an 8. But she had far too much passion, and could she tone it down a bit? This of course is an absurd scenario, and it was met with much laughter. But it is actually not too far from the truth in terms of how companies try to extract these qualities from their staff. They usually try to do it by imposing competency frameworks on people. Imagine becoming able to step up your passion to something described as a competency!

The enlightened companies understand how to bring passion, energy, flexibility, and creativity into the workplace. Notice that I didn't say that they understand how to "get these qualities." That's because they understand that they can't be "got." These qualities can't be pulled out of people on demand. People have to be supported to release them naturally and spontaneously. Creating work environments that are stimulating, honest, supportive, interesting, where people are listened to and involved— that's the only way. You simply cannot legislate or regulate for them. That's where companies and their highly paid consultant advisors are kidding themselves. And it is precisely where the enlightened companies have their eyes wide open.

WE'RE HUMANS, WE WANT MEANING

Our work is very important to us. There is so much at stake and there is so much wrapped up in work: our self-esteem, our ability to provide for ourselves and our families, our need to be acknowledged and recognized. Our work is a source of meaning for us in our lives. Human beings are the only species on the planet who strive for meaning. A life without meaning is depressing and soul-less. Many people don't get a whole lot of meaning from their work. Hopefully they get it in their relationships, their hobbies, and out-of-work pastimes instead.

If we are lucky, we can derive some kind of meaning from what we do every day. It may not be the "I want to save the world" kind. It can be much more modest than that—making a customer happy, helping out a colleague, balancing the books at the end of the day, writing a good report. The smallest things give us the slivers of meaning that are so important to us, to make us feel that we have contributed, that we are worthwhile, and that we have something to offer the world.

Our need for meaning explains why brands like Nike and Apple have become iconic. We as consumers want more than just a product, we want something we can identify with. It's the same with work. We want more than just a job. We want work that helps us to express who we are. We want to do something that makes us feel alive, that feels worthwhile for us. This is true of all of us, not just some of us. How many companies realize this, let alone acknowledge it?

THE MISSING CONVERSATION

In my entire career I have only had one conversation about what work means to me. The boss I had the conversation with is a man who understands how to get the best out of people, how to help them to feel inspired about work, and encourages them to be the best they possibly can be. People describe him as a great mentor and teacher.

If managers could do this it would release so much energy and excitement into the workplace, and would do more than the best "employee engagement" program could ever possibly do. Yet it doesn't happen.

At work we don't usually have real conversations about meaning or anything else that is of fundamental importance to us. To do so we have to be prepared to be open about ourselves and what is important to us. That feels too risky most of the time.

Real conversations are rare, but they sometimes come about when there is the threat of some crisis or other. There was a CEO of a company who had never been open and real with his executive team. He acted more like a robot at work than a human being. It was his teenage son who unintentionally plunged the CEO into honest revelation. The son had gone into work with his father on "Bring your kids to work day." The boy sat in meetings with his dad all day. Much of the time he spent looking totally bored. At the end of the last meeting of the day the CEO turned to his son and said, "So what do you think of what I do?"

The boy shrugged and replied, "Not much."

The father was indignant, and asked, "What do you mean, 'Not much'? You've been with me all day, and we've done a lot."

The son said, "All you do is talk: in meetings, on the phone, over email."

At that moment a lot was at stake for this CEO. He desperately wanted his son to be impressed by what his father did, to understand the importance of it, and also for the executives in the room to see that his son was impressed. The CEO was on the verge of a crisis. His response was, "I have to talk to people. I have to understand what is going on in the outside world, what they want from us, and what is changing. I have to translate to our inside world what they are saying, and I have to know what is happening in my company and what my people are thinking and feeling. I am chief story teller."

This boy gave his father the opportunity to describe the significance of his work in a way that he hadn't even thought of. In uttering those words he found a passion and meaning that he hadn't previously touched.

OLD FASHIONED VALUES, CUTTING-EDGE COMPANIES

These enlightened companies rarely do anything that, in and of itself, is radical. Most of what they do, the things at which those of us in more conventional organizations wonder, is actually very basic and complete common sense. This is the amazing thing. Strong values, good service, treating people with respect, and finding the best way to do a job—all these things on the surface are so obvious and simple. To those people who have strong values, they are. On one level it is bizarre that we herald these companies so much, and are so intrigued by them and what they do. What they do is so simple. We only look in awe at them because the comparison with Stone Age companies is so stark.

As we have seen, any company can be enlightened. It does not depend on what it does. It depends on what the people running these companies care about.

Even if what a company does is not particularly exciting, and the its products are not that interesting, it can still be an exciting place to work and a paragon of customer care. Fruit juices are not that exciting, but the Innocent drinks company has become something of an icon. It is a vibrant place to work, and has products that make people smile. The story of how it was first started, the way it is run, the packaging of the drinks, the customer promise, and the people who work there have all captured our imagination.

Innocent was started by a couple of friends who had had enough of their jobs in the financial sector. They thought that there might be a market for smoothies and juices. They made some and sold them at a pop festival. They had two large bins. One had a notice saying, "If you think we should give up our jobs to do this, put your empty bottle in here." The other said, "If you think we should carry on with our jobs, put your bottles in here." At the end of the day the first one was full and the other one virtually empty.

I visited Innocent in its very scruffy little premises in Shepherds Bush. As I waited lots of people passed by. Everyone was smiley and pleasant and asked me if I would like a drink. There was a real buzz about the place. I asked Richard, one of the co-founders, lots of questions about the company culture, why they had set things up as they had, how they chose people to work there, and lots of other questions. He told me he had done things in the only way he knew how. The company reflected his values. It was as simple as that and it showed.

In a way companies like Innocent have gone back to basics, to old-fashioned values. Innocent cares about its customers and does what it can to demonstrate its commitment. On the labels on its orange juice it says that it tries its best to make sure the juice is very fresh, but if customers don't agree, they should post a set of keys to Innocent, and someone will go and make them fresh orange juice in their kitchen the next day. A customer from the north of Norway decided to test Innocent on this. Sure enough, someone got on a plane, went up there the following morning and made the customer the juice.

It is this kind of ethos that sets some companies apart from the rest. It is not difficult to do what they do, but most other companies don't do it.

6

Towards a compelling future

Initiative beats inertia every time. The enlightened companies are taking action. They are putting right what is wrong about the ways their Stone Age counterparts manage. They are reinventing our notion of organizations. They are winning in the market place and they are winning the war for talent.

These companies are winning because the way they are doing business makes sense to customers who are looking for better service, more transparency in business relationships, and innovation in the products and services that they buy. It makes sense to employees who are increasingly searching for meaning in their work. They want to enjoy their work as well as feel that they are doing a good job, and they expect to be treated well at work. They create a work environment where people feel alive instead of half dead.

But more than all this, these companies are operating in a way that is honest, ethical, and decent. Old-fashioned values are making a comeback as people the world over are starting to get fed-up with the powerful, capitalist enterprise and are looking for better relationships with those they work for and those they buy from. Witness the effort that some of the big brands make to show consumers that they care. There is a massive upsurge worldwide in demand for decency and honesty. It won't go away. Organizations of the new, enlightened type will be the only ones that can satisfy our needs in the future. We want more than good products and service; we want to know that the companies we deal with have values that we can buy into.

There is no downside. There is just the ongoing need to stay fresh, be alert to changes that need to be responded to, and avoid the complacency that so often characterizes Stone Age companies.

The enlightened companies capture people's imaginations. They are rallying supporters. They are clear in their mission, overt in their values, and what they stand for appeals to the kind of people they want to work for them and with them. They are confident about what they want to achieve and what matters to them, but they don't kid themselves that there is only one way to get there. And they know it doesn't happen in a linear way. They are comfortable with uncertainty and chaos. In short, they are realistic and they see things as they are, rather than how they think they ought to be.

KEEPING IT FRESH

There are lessons to learn from these enlightened companies and their leaders. However, there is an inherent danger in examining them and trying to emulate what they do in our own companies. What we shouldn't do is try to imitate and codify what they do. That is what Stone Age companies do. Imitation of practices without living of values is shallow.

The result of codification is that practices can soon become set in stone. Once that happens the vibrancy, creativity, and passion is lost. Instead of codifying it we need to understand it. The last thing that Stone Age companies should be doing is benchmarking and looking for best practices. First, because what's right for one organization is not right for another so the notion of "best practice" is a paradoxical one. Second, because the practices that we observe happening in any organization are only the manifestation of a fundamental belief system. An analogy would be that we can observe symptoms of illness or wellness but we cannot recreate those symptoms if we don't know anything about the causes. We can't have good skin unless we know that we need to eat well, sleep, and exercise in order to get that result. The mistake that companies make in chasing best practice is the equivalent of trying to get the good skin without investing in the elements that make that possible. So, to use an example from work, we see that the great companies inspire trust and honesty so we write up some values statements about those things and stick them on the wall. Trust and honesty cannot be mandated and cannot be bought.

THE ROUTE TO ENLIGHTENMENT

There is hope. Stone Age companies can be saved. They can either take the easy route or they can continue to struggle. The route to change is not flailing around with different initiatives and change programs that make small, short-term differences—if they make a difference at all. Change only comes when these fundamentals are addressed:

1   *Know yourself*: Be clear about what you believe in.
    Bill Gore and his wife were. The key here is values.
    Ask, "What's important to me about ...?" Making
    money, advancing my career, beating the competition
    doesn't count. Providing the best service that
    customers could wish for, being the best innovators,
    making the workplace more humane do count. They
    are values. If the top person doesn't have clear
    values, the company will be rudderless.

2   *Know your passions*. Values aren't enough on their
    own. You need passion in order to create momentum
    to do things. And you need passion to inspire others.

3   *Know when to stick to your guns and when not to*.
    Don't sway from your values but do sway from your
    opinions when they are not working. Values have to be
    constant. In everything else you have to be flexible.

4   *Communicate from the heart*. Do this and you will
    attract the people who share your values. If they
    don't you will always have a struggle.

5   *Question your assumptions, always*. The day you stop
    questioning your own and others' assumptions
    (including those of your customers) is the day you
    run into the danger of getting onto that slippery
    Stone Age slope.

6   *Listen intently*. Listening is the precursor to learning.
    Listen to everyone—especially your staff and customers.

7   *Be prepared to change*. Listening and learning will
    alert you to the need to change. The ability to be flex-
    ible and to change is the key to great relationships in
    business and everywhere else in life. It's also the key
    to adaptation and survival.

TABLE 6.1 SEE THE DIFFERENCE— SPOTTING ENLIGHTENED COMPANIES

Stone Age companies	*Enlightened companies*
CUSTOMERS	
■ They put themselves first	■ They put the customers first
■ They sell them what they have	■ They get insight to understand what the customer needs
■ Customer service is seen as a process	■ Customer service is integrated into everything they do
■ They do the minimum necessary to provide *good enough* service	■ They are constantly working at improving their offer, service and communication with the customer
■ They spend more time thinking about themselves than they spend thinking about their customers	■ Everything they do is seen through a customer filter
■ Customers don't feature much in their conversations	■ All you hear when you listen in is discussion about their customers
PEOPLE	
■ They manage them as closely as possible	■ They hire talented people and give them the freedom to be creative
■ Their underlying assumption is that people can't be trusted	■ Their starting point is to trust people

- They tell them what they need to know. Communication is top down.
- They talk about values
- They see people as just another resource

- They keep everyone informed and two-way communication flows

- They live their values
- They know that people are everything

LEADERSHIP
- People are over-managed and under-led
- They manage by issuing orders and imposing control
- They assume the role of expert, not to be questioned

- They are power driven
- They are always right

- They are constantly seeking to prove themselves

- Leadership is clear and palpable but not oppressive
- They lead through conversation and involvement
- They are facilitators and encourage people to question and challenge

- They are values driven
- They admit when they are wrong
- They have nothing to prove

INNOVATION
- They tell people to be innovative

- They allow them to be innovative by encouraging risk, nurturing new ideas and giving as much space for creativity as they do for analysis

- They don't like mistakes
- They encourage experimentation and know that mistakes are necessary to learn
- They don't understand that the culture that they have created stifles innovation
- They know that they need to constantly pay attention to making sure their culture positively encourages innovation
- They don't understand it: they talk about innovation but don't realize that their behaviour discourages it
- They understand it well: they are aware of what kind of behaviour encourages and what discourages innovation

CHANGE

- They think that change is best done top-down
- They realize that real change occurs when people want to change, not because it is mandated from the top
- They have a rational and linear approach
- They have an intuitive, emergent approach
- They think that all you need to do is give people a sound rationale
- They know that you have to engage and involve people and win their hearts as well as their minds
- They look for short-term fixes
- They want to create long-term solutions

WHAT IT'S LIKE WORKING THERE

- It is stifled, stiff, and heavy
- It is vibrant, buzzing, and full of energy

- It is characterized by doing things that have been done that way for years
- Little time is spent reflecting

- Conversations are transactional

- It is normal for people to think about how things may be done differently

- Lots of time is spent reflecting on what is happening and how things might be different
- Conversations produce possibilities

I am an optimist. I believe that Stone Age companies will become rarer and rarer. I believe that the pressure is mounting and they simply can't stay the same. Something has to happen. The people who currently call the shots in Stone Age companies will become obsolete unless they change.

If you have read this far in the book you are probably not one of them. You are probably an optimist too. You are probably one of the pioneers who will be part of creating a very different type of company from the ones most of us have experienced so far. Know what you believe in and have the courage to keep on taking those steps towards a compelling future away from the Stone Age.